THE SKILL ARCHITECT

-75 LIFE SKILLS FOR EVERYONE VOLUME 3

THE SKILL ARCHITECT

© Copyright, 2021, Prasad Prakash Tupache

All rights are reserved. No part of this book may be reproduced or transmitted in any form by any means; electronic or mechanical including photography, recording, or any information storage or retrieval system; without the prior written consent of its author.

The opinions/ contents expressed in this book are solely of the author and do not represent the opinions/standings/thoughts of **Amazon Kindle Direct publication**. No responsibility or liability is assumed by the publisher for any injury, damage or financial loss sustained to a person or property by the use of any information in this book, personal or otherwise, directly or indirectly. While every effort has been made to ensure reliability and accuracy of the information within , all liability , negligence or otherwise, by any use , misuse or abuse of the operation of any method, strategy , instruction or idea contained in the material herein is the sole responsibility of the reader. Any copyright not held by the publisher are owned by their respective authors. All information in this book is generalized and presented only for the informational purpose "as it is" without warranty or guarantee of any kind.

All trademarks and brands referred to in this book are only for illustrative purpose are the property of their respective owners and not affiliated with this publication in any way. The trademarks being used without permission don't authorize their association or sponsorship with this book.

ISBN:9798539583835

Price:

Publishing Year 2021

Published and Printed by:

Independently Published through Amazon Kindle Direct Publication
Office Address: Amazon (India) , Brigade Gateway , 8Th Floor, 26/1, Dr. Rajkumar Road, Malleshwaram (W) , Bangalore -560055, Karnataka, India
Phones: +918033273000
E-mail: amznindpr@amazon.com
Website: www.Amazon.in

Printed in India

& Various International Amazon Marketplace (website) through print on demand technology

THE SKILL ARCHITECT

THE SKILL ARCHITECT

-75 LIFE SKILLS FOR EVERYONE – VOLUME 3

PRASAD PRAKASH TUPACHE.

B.E.(METALLURGY) , EPGDBM , INTERNATIONAL WELDINGTECHNOLOGIST , SIX SIGMA GREEN BELT , ASNT LEVEL II IN RT,UT,PT,VT,MT, EX.QUALITY HEAD .

INDEPENDENTLY PUBLISHED THROUGH AMAZON KINDLE DIRECT

THE SKILL ARCHITECT

WITH BEST COMPLIMENTS FROM :

M/S TUPACHE CONSULTANTS

PROPRIETOR: MR.PRASAD PRAKASH TUPACHE,

GSTIN: 27AFEPT0247H1ZF, URN: UDYAM-MH260099149,

SURVEY NO 79/20, SHIVRATNA COLONY, PACHPIR CHAUK,

KOKANE NAGAR, KALEWADI, PIMPRI, PUNE -411017

CONTACT: 9970173983

THE SKILL ARCHITECT

AUTHOR:

MR. PRASAD PRAKASH TUPACHE,

B.E.(METALLURGY) ,EPGDBM , INTERNATIONAL WELDING TECHNOLOGIST , SIXSIGMA GREEN BELT .ASNT LEVEL II IN RT,UT,PT,VT,MT,EX.QUALITY HEAD .

ADDRESS:

SURVEY NO 79/20, SHIVRATNA COLONY,PACHPIR

CHAUK, KOKANE NAGAR, KALEWADI,

PIMPRI, PUNE 411017.

FONT SETTING: MR. PRASAD PRAKASH TUPACHE.

COVER DESIGN:

MR. PRASAD PRAKASH TUPACHE.

A)FRONT PHOTO CREDIT:CANVA .COM

B) REAR PHOTO CREDIT :CANVA.COM

THE SKILL ARCHITECT

DEDICATION

PHOTO CREDIT: PROVIDENCE DOUCET, UNSPLASH.COM

THIS BOOK IS VERY VERY SINCERELY DEDICATED TO

MY DEAR,

- PARENTS
- TEACHERS
- FRIENDS
- ALL FAMILY MEMBERS
- COLLEAGUES
- PROFESSIONALS
- WORKMEN & OPERATORS
- EVERY READER

AND LAST BUT NOT LEAST

- TO MY LOVELY KIDS!

THANKS A LOT FOR YOUR CONSTANT BELEIEF!

THE SKILL ARCHITECT

PHOTO CREDIT: MAHESH, UNSPLASH.COM

Dear Friends,

Good Morning & Seasons Greeting!

It gives me immense pleasure to present my new English book – **The Skill Architect – 75 Life Skills for Every One, Volume 3 with** *all of you!* This moment is special!
With completion of two volumes, we thoughtfully moved to writing of third volume. Here our main focus was to simplify the difficult situations of life and give reader a confident and firm reading experience!

With these thought process, we started writing and with Bappa's blessing, we could make it through! In This book, we are providing, sharing of useful experiences, competitive skills and general importance of adaptability to different cultures!

We hope you love & enjoy this book! Happy Reading!

THE SKILL ARCHITECT

PHOTO CREDIT: AMELIE NIKLAS, UNSPLASH.COM

Dear Friends,

"The Skill Architect -75 Life Skills for Every One, Volume 3" has apt illustrations in the form of number of pictures and images.

The main resource of these images is internet.

The images are downloaded for free with photo credit mentioned to its creator in respective photo as it found appropriate.

We herewith sincerely thank all respected contributors on unsplash.com for their true support and creativity.

These images made me clarify the subject in easiest way! Thanks Again!

Yours Sincerely,

Prasad Prakash Tupache.

THE SKILL ARCHITECT

◆ INSPIRATIONAL ◆

IMAGE CREDIT: JANNES GLAS, UNSPLASH.COM

THE SKILL ARCHITECT

◆ INSPIRATIONAL ◆

IMAGE CREDIT: JENNY HILL, UNSPLASH.COM

THE SKILL ARCHITECT

SKILL INDEX

SR.NO	SKILL NAME	PAGE NO
151	ALMA MATTER RELATIONSHIP	3-6
152	HUMANITY	7-10
153	IMAGINATION	11-14
154	DIVERSE WORKFORCE UNDERSTANDING	15-18
155	MULTITASKING	19-22
156	EASE OF DOING	23-26
157	PERFECTION	27-30
158	SCRUTINY	31-34
159	DATA INTERPRETATION	35-38
160	OPPORTUNITY RECOGNITION	39-42
161	LEARNING THROUGH MISTKAE	43-46
162	CAPACITY ENHANCEMENT	47-50
163	SPACE MANAGEMENT	51-54
164	DESIGNER	55-58
165	NEATNESS	59-62
166	ACCURACY BUILDING	63-66
167	ERROR SENSING	67-70
168	MULTIPLE CONCEPT APPLICATION	71-74
169	FUNDAMENTAL KNOWLEDGE	75-78
170	DIRECTION BUILDING	79-82
171	APPROACH BUILDING	83-86
172	OPTION MAKING	87-90
173	TECHNICAL SOUNDNESS	91-94
174	EXPERIMENTATION	95-98
175	CONCLUSION	99-102
176	FACE READING	103-106
177	BODY LANGAUGE	107-110
178	HANDSHAKE	111-114
179	DEALING WITH UNCERTAINITY	115-118
180	PLEASANT INTERACTION	119-122

THE SKILL ARCHITECT

SKILL INDEX

SR.NO	SKILL NAME	PAGE NO
181	SUPPORT	123-126
182	EXTRA VALUE ADDITION	127-130
183	MIS CREATION	131-134
184	RATING CREATION	135-138
185	GENERAL KNOWLEDGE	139-142
186	EXHIBITION BOOTH SETTING	143-146
187	INNOVATION	147-150
188	STATUS QUO QUESTIONING	151-154
189	NOW OR NEVER ATTITUDE	155-158
190	PRACTICAL BELIEF	159-162
191	ORAL CALCULATIONS	163-166
192	PROOF GENERATION	167-170
193	LEGAL IMPACT	171-174
194	CONTROL	175-178
195	AUTHORITY EXERTION	179-182
196	RENOVATION	183-186
197	ACCOUNT KEEPING	187-190
198	BUDGETING	191-194
199	PROVISIONING	195-198
200	LIASONING	199-202
201	ENVIRONMENT SENSING	203-206
202	STRICTNESS	207-210
203	OPENNESS	211-214
204	COMPASSION	215-218
205	KINDNESS	219-222
206	CLEVERNESS	223-226
207	ESCAPE	227-230
208	INVESTMENT	231-234
209	STOCK MARKET	235-238
210	ASSURANCE	239-242

THE SKILL ARCHITECT

SKILL INDEX

SR.NO	SKILL NAME	PAGE NO
211	DEFINING	243-246
212	STEP CREATION	247-250
213	PLANNING	251-254
214	CORRECTION	255-258
215	SUGGESTION	259-262
216	IMPROVEMENT MAKING	263-266
217	TRACKING	267-270
218	EMOTIONAL INTELLIGENCE	271-274
219	STRENGTH BUILDING	275-278
220	FLEXIBILITY	279-282
221	LARGER THAN LIFE	283-286
222	MOVIE & PLAY WATCHING	287-290
223	FORT & HISTORY LIKING	292-296
224	GEOGRAPHICAL COMFORT	297-300
225	FORGETTING	301-303

PREFACE : IDEA OF THIS BOOK

Dear Friends,

Good Morning and welcome to the simple and easy book onskill development!

It gives me immense pleasure to write this preface after completion of writing this book! The preface is about thegeneral introduction about the book and its content, the situations experienced while writing various chapters, the state of mind at different stages of book creation and finally the satisfaction it gave me after completing the task in 61 days with 3 different volumes of this book each comprising 75 skills!

As we all know the skills are main difference makers in today's highly competitive and expanding world. When two candidates with equal qualification and experience are thought up for the single important executive position, it is the skill that decides the right choice.

Qualification has identity of technical and academic compatibility to role desired. Experience has recognition Of Staying firm in the field for several years with taste of success and challenges together. This

THE SKILL ARCHITECT

is why we say experience is the best teacher. But apart from the qualification and experience the ease with which we master our work is always known as skill!

We like tea, but we like a particular brand very much! We like to watch cricket, but we support only few players beyond our normal excitement. We like to travel, but some places always attract us to visit often? What makes it so so special! It's the beauty of the taste of the tea, the thrill of cricket certain player exhibit in the game of cricket and the divine comfort of place where we love to visit often.

Skill has such affinity to draw your customers, visitors, critics to commonly declare you as the best performer of any typical art & science. The commerce automatically follows when you keep reinventing your skills!

Noting the importance of the skills in today's life, on 26 Th Jan, 2021, I have listed 225 Skills which are generally important and necessary. Then by creating rough plan for execution started writing of this book. Every stage of this book is a wonderful re learning for me. When the format and plot of the content become familiar, the speed is picked up and by daily completion of 6-7 chapters, we could complete this book in 61 days in 3 different volumes!

The attempt is made to suggest suitable illustrations and here internet image resource done the fantastic task. The idea to have access to such numerous illustrations is simply awesome and it has shown great support to an author's creativity and experimentation.

Typical challenging phases did come while writing this book which involved too much thinking on certain topic, how to start a particular skill and how it should be kept engaging, how to put genuine real life examples which will help to understand the subject in easiest way, how to ponder thought upon a difficult skill when there are considerable technicalities involved, all these challenges are overcome with all possible determination, patience and belief on self and almighty. This makes me able to complete the book in reasonable good time as per my own understanding.

Being the second book, the experience of writing was comparatively easy and I have witnessed improved confidence after writing every 100 pages in about weeks' time! The satisfaction of going through this numerical journey was awesome and achieving 900 pages Was a big personal satisfaction while on the go. We have tried our best to present the most practical experiences to make this book user friendly. The narration used here is simple, easy and readable. We have taken care to highlight special paragraph from the skill chapters to emphasize certain aspects of the chapter easily!

Friends, every creation has its own accomplishment and its own limits. Human element always plays the role of constant improvement and thoughtful revision of what can be done more to make it more easy and simple. We are aware that there may be certain shortfalls, some errors or some different opinions 180 degree opposite! But friends, please let us share with you that individuality, freedom and experimentation has always convinced me to go ahead and put the skill details in front of you to have easy and simple understanding.

In case of any concern or if some thoughts found to be too bold, we can always discuss for more clarification. We have tried our best to think in depth before putting it for you!

Hope you all like this book! We wish you happy reading!

Yours Friendly

– Prasad Prakash Tupache.

LETS START

THE SKILL ARCHITECT

SKILL 151 : ALMA MATTER RELATIONSHIP SKILL

PHOTO CREDIT : SPENCER RUSSEL, UNSPALSH .COM

Dear Friends,

Good Morning and welcome to yet another skill chapter- Alma matter relationship skill. Let's go into the details.

> " *Education has its own importance in our life. Education give us the power to think , act and improve as per the right way! Alma matter develops our thinking in early age!*"

THE SKILL ARCHITECT

College life is an important phase in a bachelor's life. The ability to learn, think, experiment, discuss and enjoy the learning develops in these years. Alma matter, the institute from where we receive our lifetime degree and on the basis of which we work in society to earn a respectable living is always an inspiration. Let us see the important skill of engagement with this Alma matter post completing your education.

Alma matter relationship:

- It's always fascinating to remain in touch with an institute from where you receive your degree. You have lots of friends who become executives in their career in different organizations and you have future student who can get the chance to serve for different organizations when they network with their seniors. In this way, relation with Alma matter is great way of building professional relationship.
- Number of research project is carried out in reputed institutes. When industry expert their views and experience, it become easy platform of continuous improvement.
- Industry is meant for profit while institutes are established to spread knowledge to improve quality of life of individual. A touch with Alma matter always reminds you the project you carried out in your yester years.
- Many times in life when we stuck in life, visiting your Alma matter gives you courage to understand the situations and work for every possible solution.

- When we study establishment of several organizations, we find there is huge possibility that founder of the organizations were knowing each other for quite a time which builds their relation and this personal relation got converted into sound professional relation . It is not required that you remain in touch every day, however it is important to remain friendly whenever you meet in future life. This is simple teaching one get from Alma matter.
- Relations are backbone of success and relation provides us insight about realities of life. When we study in college, many people come together to discuss issues, resolve problem and find out a solution under the guidance of your teachers. In professional environment, you have to think on possibilities of people coming together to make big things together. In this system everyone protects interest of each stakeholder. When such association works together they deliver wonderful products. The start of such relation start with opportunities you receive in your almamatter.
- There is gentle way to resolve issues with friendly discussion and in depth analysis. Such group discussion is done in early phase of life in your Alma matter. At work , you may met with a colleague who is twenty years senior to you but when you both know you are from same institute, the sharing become easy as you share same culture hence most of way of learning and working are same which make it easy to work together.
- What if person working in organization hails from different institutes and they have to deliver a high

potential project? In any organization, selection happens with certain preset value requirement. The selection is done from college which is having certain grades and accreditation. When you have such grades, then it is certain that student coming from such institute will have a high entry merit which other may not have! The quality of their project may be far futuristic than other students, the grooming happened and extracurricular skill acquired may be far greater that other, this comparative benefits ensure when you joins from accredited institutes, you have these qualifications which help you to deliver with comfort. Hence such student gets easily gel up in any type of teams!

- With increased use of social networking now it is become very easy to find out jobs. If you know your friend in organization, he may help you to become familiar with internal environment, opportunities available, risks associated with certain sections, this helps you to take joining decision with caution. Alma matter relation is always beneficial. Always cherish this relation!

Hope you like this chapter! Let's pause here!✍

SKILL 152 : HUMANITY SKILL

PHOTO CREDIT : PASCAL BERNARDO, UNSPLASH.COM

Dear Friends,

Good afternoon and welcome to yet another skill chapter – Humanity skill. Let's go into the details!

> *"Humanity is a genuine concern of brotherhood, mutual respect, and friendly co-operation to fosterthe spirit of symbiosis! It connects people!"*

When it comes to dealing with people. The humanity skill plays very very important role. Humanity is all about knowing the person with love, trust, care and their well-being. Humanity means supporting a person in crisis and shares your knowledge when he seeks some guidance from you. Let's us see various humanity skill aspect point wise!

Humanity Skill Aspects:

Stay humane, be humane, and understand human needs!

- Humanity does not require financial help always, a little bit of extended support, a little bit appreciation and a little bit care helps to build human relation.
- It is strange but true that when we are living in friends circle, not everyone has same financial condition nor we have same cultural background. We come there with natural affection and do our study or work together. Be it a matter of knowing study concept, be it a matter of getting work done we require each other's participation, cooperation. Just cooperate two people and see how many people will co-operate with you. Resolve the problems of two people and see what kind of support you receive from your friends circle. When you selflessly do good things for others, it creates a positive energy in the surrounding and it get occupied

the space in which you work or study. This is the basic power of humanity which makes things simple and easy to relate.

- It is strange feeling that only weak people need help and strong people can solve their problem on their own. This is wrong statement and everyone has to take help of someone at some part of time. People can buy resources by spending money but people get good co-operation only when they deal with people with mutual trust and brotherhood.
- Many complex issues get resolved when we carefully observe the things, we work on its remedy, we discuss alternatives of getting things done, we share these alternative in group and then we get various views on those alternatives, we divide activities and own certain activities, this way our work become simple and with united efforts we achieve what we want .This is nothing but strength of humanity.
- Have you ever wondered how the macro organization works so efficiently? There are thousand and lakhs teaming members working and yet they work with efficiency and result. How this is possible to control so many people same time? Friends, it's so simple. Strong value culture and respect for every individual make you work in synergy, unity and integrity. Humanity here resolves doubts through discussions, humanity offer help in critical situations; humanity help to fill the gap between

interpersonal relations, such macro organizations have strict performance policies and perfectly informal working environment. It means as far as you keep your customer happy and content, it okay if you arrive little late because of traffic or it is okay if you stay there for long hours till completion of your that days target. You get your reward and much time you are appreciated for the generosity you show in your performance. This is completely human inspiration to dedicate yourself at work and stay committed.

- In a hardworking culture lot of value get inherited. A farmer will work for more than twelve hours, a doctor can offer their duty 24 x7, and an Engineer will put long working hours when critical installations are being installed. All these professions have one thing in common – commitment to humanity. Farmers do hard work to feed the population, doctors devote their every minute to save patient life and keep them away from diseases, Engineers work hard to save consumption of natural resources and provide comfort to human being by developing product and services that simplifies normal working. A soldier commits his life to protect his people from external attacks. Social workers resolves people problem and make their life humane. Humanity is serving each other with mutual affection without expecting any return. Hope you like this chapter. Humanity is selfless service! Let's pause here!

SKILL 153 : IMAGINATION SKILL

PHOTO CREDIT : TETIANA SHYSHKINA, UNSPLASH.COM

Dear Friends,

Good Evening and welcome to yet another skill chapter imagination skill! Let's go into the details!

> *"Imagination is special ability to think for different perspectives, identify new looks and arrange things in altogether different manner just to present a stunning picture of achievements!"*

When we thought about the circle, we invented wheel. When we thought about line, we developed roads. When we thought about structure of walls supported with roof, we constructed towers! Friends, what is so common in these achievements? It's the power of imagination which makes us try different things with different perspective and finally achieving the desired picture of imaginary concept. Let us see, how the imagination skill is developed in various professions all around the globe.

The Journey of Imagination in different professions:

- When a painter think about the imagination, different combinations of colour scheme are tried out. At one particular experiment, he achieves the desired texture, the desired stroke of brush and the system of things which are kept and arranged to please our eyes & senses.
- When an engineer imagines a scientific concept to reality, they combine different principles with fixed calculations to provide unbelievable result. Look first car is designed, and then they installed Hi-Fi music system, then Wi-Fi connectivity arrived, then remote control & GPRS tracking, then different combinations of fuel and enhanced economy! This is the way how imagination took its shape in its development sequence. The constant quest of trying out different ideas on practically possible options make imagination work in all its good form. It is the

power of imagination which has proved its mettle in developing various cost effective product for the benefit of mankind!

- When a musician applies his imagination, he composes different tunes out of nothing. He has support of basic tunes and well-crafted words, in this combination he weave various sound notes to deliver a fresh melodious song. It is his imagination that who will play what and for how much time. This plotting is shear contribution of dedicated efforts made by the team of musicians.
- When artist tries different stuffs, they always think for out of the box experiments. Many of these experiments are prone to failure because of unavailability of right knowledge, its application and its overall impact. This is the development phase. In this phase artist faces extreme challenges to make their design work as per their final imaginary product. The number of changes made in design during construction paves out possibility of new product idea strangely. In the field of imagination, it is happened many times that you search something for long time and instead you find something very very special and unbelievable. But to attain such discoveries you have to always explore the area which is new for your imagination.
- The ability to challenge the status quo is basic requirement to have ultimate imagination. When we imagined can energy of sun used to heat water,the solar energy equipment is evolved.

- When we thought about possibility of using power of wind to move turbines, we developed wind mills. When we imagined can metals be mixed with each other and what will be their result, we got number of alloy development which made discovery of special purpose machines at low cost.
- The concept of imagination goes through several failures. Before public acceptance of an actor he may have to go through number of flops till his role is liked by public. He portrays imaginary characters which may appeal the audience and support the story or may not suit the story. The attention is sought out only after complete matching of character with storyline. This is the moment when imagination becomes a successful character. When the role becomes hit, people know that particular actor for that role for his lifetime, but till it become a hit, he has to face several failures.
- Imagination is ever expanding concept and people try out different combinations of their knowledge, skill, practical experience to create a totally new product or service. Fashion and imagination has close association. Various ideas are tried out in fashion design and they become trend when liked by masses. Before a fashion design clicks, it has to go through several trials on different models. The perfect suit has best outfit and best model.

Hope you like this chapter. Let's pause here! ✍

SKILL 154 : DIVERSE WORKFORCE UNDERSTANDING SKILL

PHOTO CREDIT : ALEX KOTLIARSKYI, UNSPLASH.COM

Dear Friends,

Good Morning and welcome to yet another skill chapter- Diverse workforce understanding skill. Let's go into the details.

> *"You visit the workplace and note different activities. People interacting in shop floors have different skillsets while people working in office and site has different skillsets. You need to work with diversity with ease!"*

Workforce and work pressure is something special concern when we work in certain environment. People have different skillset, attitudes, experience and zeal to carry out things. When we join a workplace, we need to understand these basic facts about diversity at work place. What will happen if we work with samespeed and process everywhere? Things will not work out!

If you are working for production you have to always think about getting job completed in time. If you are working for quality assurance and control , you have to always think for how this job can be delivered with accuracy and detailed clarity .When you are working on sites there is always hurry to set things right while there may be follow up if some material is not received in time . At such environments, you need to understand the intentions with which people are working .This is about diverse workforce understanding skill. Let's see point wise how this skill can be mastered.

Diverse workforce understanding skill:

- Learn your role and the people regularly interacting with you. Discuss the normal work practices and expectation from your role.
- Every environment has safe working practices. Learn the rules and follow these rules.
- People may have come from different backgrounds, different country and different regions. They may have different culture and different food habits. But

One thing is common with them all – the ability to gel with knowledge and humbleness. Humbleness make them work with positive approach, dedication andcommitment.

- We have to treat everyone with respect and maximum attention one can give to their concerns. Patient listening helps to increase engagement and make things happen at work.
- Sometime a diverse workforce consist of team of professionals having different skillsets and inclination. When such talented team is formed, there are chances of different opinions and views about looking at same thing with different vision. Here the role of the team leader is to agree for certain point and discuss clearly about points of disagreements.
- When we are working on cross country project with different time zone, if a common understanding is set we can work with major job requirement, joint challenges and actions that will yield results. Trust is the basic factor when we want to work with people from different regions. We have to follow what we have said. This is the minimum expectation people expect from us. If things does not happen as per their expectation, people wait for another chance but repeat nonperformance is not acceptable. In diverse workforce, we respect each other's commitment and allow some time to know and understand our role requirement. When you give some time for professional relations, you gain

valuable support from different people during future course of time.

- Wherever we work, time, urgency, errors and understanding will remain same. When people get enough maturity about their work, they adjust things informally. It means when the delivery is urgent, people stay for long hours and ensure the work is done on time. When there are errors during construction, people understand the reason of error and correct the things. When there are role changes, transfer and promotions, people give respect required for every position along with enhanced authority level. Handling promotion is one of the critical adjustment skills. You have to work with same people and to maintain same work spirit without showing your attitude of being promoted. Generally authority is exhibited through performance. You can have same friendly relations and yet you can hold your authority. It's all about people management.
- When you donate your time for developing people, after some time you get wonderful returns in the form of increased support. Depending upon the difficulty level at work you may work together or you may work at respective sites. Clear communication, instant rapport and good work ethics make your things smooth and clear. In such environment, it is very very easy to work with success!

Hope you like this chapter! Let's pause here!

SKILL 155 : MULTITASKING SKILL

PHOTO CREDIT : MATT BERO , UNSPLASH.COM

Dear Friends,

Good afternoon and welcome to yet another skill chapter – Multitasking skill. Let's go into the details.

> *"Multitasking is all about managing number of things in least amount of time. It's about parallel working. To increase workforce efficiency, avenues of multitasking must be found out!"*

Let's see few practical situations where you need to multitask!

Multitasking Situations:

- Generally the role of a quality engineer requires visiting in process job for their completeness, reporting the status of inspecting authorities and completion of supporting inspection report. In a particular work environment, either it a line production or project environment, number of activities are going on in series and parallel. You have to identify the series activities and decide their optimum sequence as per set procedure
- Then you can review parallel task which can be done with ongoing work. The observation period of series activity is used for carrying out parallel activity. This is about managing your work area by doing multitasking.
- Suppose in a fabrication shop, if you inspect the set up and give clearance for further processing, people will complete that work, now you have time to check for other test if they are ready else you can go for documentation of inspected things to make thing easy for next day. When tests are carried out, you need to stay there and observe the test, record the result and document it properly. During this observation period, you cannot carry out any other activity else you will not able to find out variation during test. Hence a critical evaluation of activities is necessary.
- When you are working in preparation of an event, you have to do lots of multitasking. You have to decide

schedule, you have to communicate to service providers to arrange things, you have to send invitations, you have to arrange guest and decide their right felicitation. While doing this you have to take care of your daily work. Here your time management skill work well along with multitasking.

- Multitasking is also referred to work done on computer. We work in several programs same time. Because of multitasking window, we get easy reference of things and because of which we can take quick decisions. The accuracy of our decision depends upon the accuracy of data we receive. Hence it is important, when we collecting data, it should be authentic and can be easily relatable.
- The basic aspect before hiring a candidate is his ability to have diverse qualification. When you have multiple qualification and certification, you can work on so many things efficiently. You can direct others about how the work is done. How things to be handled and what is the result of a good teamwork. When you are mutlitasker and a leader, you exactly know where to put your efforts and energy to make things workable. You can see, people join organization at entry stage and as they progresses they acquire much needed skill to become a multi taskers. In less amount of time they achieve good hold on their work and hence become successful at early age.
- Some person has multiple talent and they can manage different things same time. This is achieved by continuous practice and determination. Have you ever wondered to see an engineer who can sing well, a

doctor who play a guitar in style, a policeman giving motivational speech or a teacher engaged in development of garden in his backyard? These are all examples of good hold on multitasking with multiskilling.
- In career also, people get various certification as they become senior in their service. This involve various diplomas, certification entrance exams, various training programs and seminars, international project presentation contest and various scientific exhibitions. Through all these means professional work on their career goal to achieve great heights. The time required to carry out these activities is earned by increasing expertise in daily task or practicing serial and parallel way of multitasking.
- Multitasking directly adds to profit as you can do number of things with the support of same team, also as you work on different project, you apply these skills to cut short the time required to complete activity. Multitasking is much in demand skill and it is the best way to achieve great heights in your career and in personal life.

Hope you like this chapter! Let's pause here!

SKILL 156 : EASE OF DOING SKILL

PHOTO CREDIT : MARTIN MAGNEMYR, UNSPLASH.COM

Dear Friends,

Good Evening and welcome to yet another skill chapter- the ease of doing skill. Let's go into the details!

> *"Ease of doing make things fast, simple and inclusive. Many people operate the system and it becomes symbol of effectiveness!"*

THE SKILL ARCHITECT

- When we find software carrying out financial transaction with rapid speed, we get amazed with technological advances. You have to input your data, software will process it and you will get your desired output within fraction of minute. Earlier when we need to carry out transactions , we have to carry out lots of manualcalculations , these calculations always has some form of manual errors , there is always a risk of missed formulae because of which whole set of calculations may go wrong. All these hurdles are simplified because of developed software's.

- Earlier machines used to have analogue control panels where the accuracy and minute recording was missing. When digital control panels arrived,accuracy of recording is increased along with ease of noting parameters up to certain decimal points.

- Ease of doing require constant practice of assigned work. When you invest certain number of hours in particular activity you get good hand at it and you become seasoned to use that equipment or machine. Once you achievemastery over its usage, you can play it as you like. This is the advantage of ease of doing.

- Jigs and fixture design is another form of ease of doing things. When you want to produce large number of certain assembly part. Let's say 1000 number; you don't prepare 1000 parts with different workmanship standard. To have consistency and uniformity what you do , you design its jig and holding fixture in which cut sub parts are assembled as per given dimensions and Then tightened and welded to provide distortion free assembly part.Here once your welding is completed, you remove the part from fixture and keep it in finished good are. Large scale Reproducibility is achieved with the help of such jigs & fixtures.

- Preparation of certificate is another important example of ease of doing things. In a certificate allotment, there is fixed content describing the certification details and certificate issuing authority, what changes is name of candidate and their registration number. With specific software, when we input certain name and details, we get print ready certificate. With such software, we can print 1000 certificate in least amount of time.

- Earlier different internal transactions were carried out with the help of paper indenting and manual entry. With latest ERP software's now one can easily integrate, send and encrypt the business data to produce clear financial records. With the enhanced use of software and application lots of registrations, applications, form filling become simple and easy to use. This method has increased the transparency of the system.

- In latest drawing and design, many supporting instructions are given to make things easy during actual construction. This involve reference of tolerance table, instruction about welding symbol and their pictorial representation, number of test to be carried out, various sectional views with which items can be seen from different angles , the nomenclature and identification of parts on drawing details by which part can be easily refereed with reference of tolerance table, instruction about welding symbol and their pictorial representation, number of test to be carried out, various sectional views with which items can be seen from different angles, the nomenclature and identification of parts on drawing details by which part can be easily refereed with respective bill of material. Because of detailed drawings, you don't need to ask second time about drawing clarity and work can be carried out almost seamlessly. Now with the help of advanced graphic scheme one can get 3D view of part to be constructed because of which dimension, orientation and bird's eye view of part can be easily visualized. This make construction work easy.

• Preparation of construction document dossier also has a standard template format. When you construct number of different project, you have to invest huge amount of time in its documentation. Documents remains long time and hence they need to be accurate and legible. To make this happen, we prepare templates of various certificates and go on filling necessary details. When bunch of documents are complied, it gives us a ready folder. Now most of the documents are sent as digital copies, so with the help of compliers number of files can be stored and send to respective client making documentation process digital, legible and reproducible.

Hope you like it! Let's pause! ✍

SKILL 157 : PERFECTION SKILL

PHOTO CREDIT : JUAN PABLO, UNSPLASH.COM

Dear Friends,

Good Evening and welcome to yet another skill chapter – Perfection skill! Let's go into the details!

> *"Creating things from scratch and making it style symbol is perfection! Working hard for achieving minute details is perfection! Failing many times till achieving desired result is perfection!"*

- How many times we get stunned to see exact expressions on a wax statue? It's nothing but several hours of practice done to create exceptional expression and fine details.
- What is the magic of magic shows performed in front of thousand spectators? It is the practice of hundred hours to simplify the skit and make it presentable in stunning manner.
- Behind every highly sold book or a hit movie, there is thousand hours practice to create interesting ideas and write funny characters. These characters talk with the people through their typical narrative style and people find them easily relatable. The exact success of creative characters is result of thousand hour practice of actors and directors to make every shot aesthetically appealing and real.
- The habit of continuous success in cricket is developed with continuous efforts, number of experiments, frequent innovations and integration of various ideas. When this mixture is combined together, we work with synergy and deliver good result. We remember teams which has maintained their track record of winning by preparing well before the match, they sweat out hard to make every playing shot safe to score runs, they work on field placement and run saving strategies to restrict the opposition in least scores, when they come for bat, they always ensure the score board is ticking, the playing eleven is combination of fast bowlers who can bowl really fast, opening batsman who can score fast, middle order batsman who can take

charge of situation at any point of time , with such combination and regular practice , one can achieve the desired consistency and maintain their number one position with perfection , hard work and determination.

- Athlete's record shows thousand hours of practice. Be it a sprint or relay, every athlete put 100% of his efforts to make things happen. We see the difference between winner and runner up is hardly fraction of second; hence it requires exact perfection in setting your game plan to decide your strategy of entering into competitionand become a winner.
- Perfection of a weight lifter is seen from the successive steps in which they increase the weight. The stamina, power and continuity is seen by number of attempts made by them before becoming a winner. There are risk that you may not able to hold the weight for long hours or it may happen that in middle of the things, you get physical injuries. You have to cross these hurdles by putting perfect efforts.

Machining of component is one of the most important perfect activity. While designing a tool cut, you have to take care of setting of job in machine jaws, setting it moment and setting parameters accurately to achieve required depth and surface finish of component. When the design tolerance is very very stringent, you have to stand there to see how tool moves on complete periphery. If the tool is not moving freely, you have to immediately fine tune your parameters to ensure correct cut. The exact result is achieved when you achieve the skill level to move machine within stipulated time. This skilled handling is the base of perfect cut.

- Learning language requires great amount of perfection. When you want to learn a new language, you have to understand its grammar first, then different part of speeches and then conversation style. As you see various media you understand of practical uses of language. When you start conversing with friends, you get good grip of that language. This way we achieve perfection in new language.

- Perfection is a valued skill. The price of item substantially increases when people note the clear aesthetics and fine details. The quality of product is rated depending upon the fine details. This fineness is achieved with meticulous planning and execution. The time factor has important connection with perfection. Earlier it takes number of hours to shape up the things, but once you achieve the perfection, your time of doing things reduces and you become fine skilled person to perform repeat tasks with desired accuracy.

Hope you like this chapter. Perfection is great identity of skilled labour which need to be respected and rewarded.

Let's pause! ✍

SKILL 158 : SCRUTINY SKILL

PHOTO CREDIT : HUDSON HINTZE , UNSPLASH.COM

Dear Friends,

Good morning & welcome to yet another skill chapter- scrutiny skill. Let's go into the details.

> *"Truth and its verification is important part of business transaction. The process of scrutiny is examination of subject matter in full depth to ensure its righteousness."*

Scrutiny ensures availability of required documents in prescribed format. The purpose of getting required document is to establish authorized proof which can be co-related with facts. Let's see the typical situations where the scrutiny is important.

Situations where scrutiny is important:

• Generally scrutiny is done before allowing for any permission. It is factual review and examination of presented truth to actual truth. If any difference is observed, it is highlighted as discrepancy and same is corrected by providing necessary justification. When we fill application for entrance examination, before appearing for examination , all given details are verified with respect to valid record in the form of available certificates . If any question is there, same is asked to resolve. People can have issue about wrong entry of marks, incomplete application, irrelevant application and application without necessary proof. Here scrutiny committee goes into details to ensure all application details are correct and if not same is rejected.

• Vendor services have become common now. While approving vendors, physical visit to his workplace is very much important. When a vendor applies for a registration code with respective organization thorough their official channel, he has to provide details about his business entity along with necessary documents. When the officials found document in line with requirement they carry out physical visit to ensure the facts. In this visit they review the working space availability, free space availability, workforce and machines availability, competency of people and the quality of their products, quality and safety management system. Based on the actual observation and supplied document they decide the approval. This scrutiny helps the vendor to ensure their registration with firm and hence work order for respective work.

- Admissions to school also follow stringent scrutiny. Which involve birth certificate, caste certificate, income certificate, district or state change certificate, any additional quota or reservation certificate? Why this is done? Just to ensure everyone get benefit of education in a justified way. No capable student should remain away from quality education. The purpose of reservation and quota is nothing but equal opportunity to every talented person and respect for service to nation. In scholarship grants and project grants, scrutiny is very very important. In scrutiny we receive details of person through authorized caste and income certificates issued by competent authorities with which the ability to qualify for scholarship is assessed and same is granted. Now because of this scrutiny and timely help, one can complete their education and achieve their degrees to progress further.

- When we dispatch the material and when it reaches the customer gate, the documents are scrutinized to ensure correct supply. During transit, many unexpected thing can happen. Which involve part damage, theft, miss out? To ensure we get required material, the consignment is unloaded with scrutiny of its packing list, verification of its part numbers and then checking their weight. When all these things are verified then the respective goods received document is cleared and same is sent to finance for bill payment to its supplier as per policy guidelines. What will happen if material is not as per requirement? Same is sent back to supplier as per agreement or supplier will suggest to check with third party for its root cause and subsequent correction or they may repair inside factory and accrue some charge for rework . Hence detail verification is important to accept the material when it is received at your gate.

- The purpose of scrutiny is to validate the truth. When there is certainty of truth, we can rely on its performance. There are minimum chances of that part or service will not behave incorrectly. If you miss verification of any incorrect point, same will enter in your system and may cause other problems which were not present in the system earlier. To avoid the same scrutiny is important.

Hope you like this chapter. Let's pause here!

SKILL 159 : DATA INTERPRETATION SKILL

PHOTO CREDIT : MARKUS SPISKE , UNSPLASH.COM

Dear Friends,

Good morning and welcome to yet another skill chapter – Data interpretation skill! Let's go into the details!

> *"Data interpretation is all about understanding the relationship between variables and make accurate decisions to influence desired change!"*

THE SKILL ARCHITECT

Data is new fuel. It moves decision making process. Decisions influence actions and actions represent movement. Movement cause changes in the system and system take care of universal well-being to lead a happy, successful and proud life! When we understand this relation we handle data with care, caution and convenience. Let's see various practical situations in which data interpretation skill simplify decision making process.

Data Interpretation Examples:

When we want to carry out various surveys, we want to find the general inclination of masses and suitability of our product to fulfill that requirement. When a survey is carried out for 100 homes to determine their choice of toothpaste, you will receive various answers from these owners. When you accumulate complete data and mark it perfectly, depending on frequency you can group it according to brands mentioned. You will find the number one brand and subsequently other brands. Based on this data, you will find the reason of popularity ofcertain brand. Now if you want to increase sell of your product, you have to increase volume of content, reduce the price of your pack, carry out expensive endorsement programme to project your product and find out the result after several month. If you notice boost in your sales by certain percentage compared to last record, you have achieved the right result of earlier data interpretation. This is simple mathematical approach to improve your sales amidst stringent competition.

- Establishment of a food processing unit follows various pre installation surveys to collect data on type of people & overall population, their average per capita income, the general lifestyle of people, education level and future plan. When such parameters are collected for particular territory, it gives you idea about the general inclination. Now when you cross check the data with the capacity of your processing plant, you can derive the production level, sales potential and financial cycle efficiency. This is the reason why sugar mills are set in area vicinity to sugarcane farm and metallurgical industries are set in the vicinity of minerals & mines. Food processing unit are set in the vicinity of city so that the product distribution will be easy. Inside city, there is huge requirement of fast food and hence to fulfill a certain typical brand, you carry out survey, analyses the responses and then decide your product launch programme. You meet with distributors and wholesalers, offer them descent commission for sales of your product and thus you set your product in desired market. This knowledge of decision making based on data plays significant role in managing business up and downs. The continuous profitability of business is result of accurate data based decisions.
- Inside facility when you wanted to carry out reduction in various cost, you carry out number of consumption studies. These studies give you a gross and detailed idea about actual requirement of raw material or manpower and its current usage. When you tabulate these findings, you will be able to understand why the consumption of raw material is increased. You

may notice , your machine is consuming more fuel and hence it needs repair , you will note work done by specific people show less output so you can separately discuss with them about their problems , you will find the specific design of product result more wastage so you can plan your design change which ensure appropriate waste saving . To take such decisions studies help you! Numbers of improvement projects are always carried out based on data interpretation. For a certain observation period, you study the process in detail and find out the gap between expected output and observed output. People cooperate with you when they notice your sincerity and hence they plug the error points highlighted by you. On successful completion of your study, you observe the change in result and this proves your point in assuring the desired cost reduction and enhanced profit based on data interpretation. The decisions prove to be valid for long time when data based approach is practiced.

Hope you like this chapter! Let's pause here!

SKILL 160 : OPPORTUNITY RECOGNITION SKILL

PHOTO CREDIT : PAUL SKORUPSKAS , UNSPLASH.COM

Dear Friends,

Good Morning and welcome to yet another skill chapter- opportunity recognition skill! Let's go into the details.

> *"Opportunities exist everywhere. It is the keen eye to surrounding that make the selection of right opportunity easy. Networking, capability and positive expression of your personality is key!"*

Friends, we see when one get instant job before completion of his bachelors, how it feels to start the career. This is nothing but appropriate reward for your talent. What if you don't get a job even after one year post graduation? It may be because you miss critical labels, important marks or influential personality. You go on giving interviews and receive feedback. Sometimes even feedbacks are also not given. To find out the right job you go on searching and on one fine day you met with the right opportunity. You prepare well for that interview. You remain fully confident in that interview and answer questions carefully and to the satisfaction of your interviewing team. This approach helps you to land over a decent job. Friends, this is all about meeting with right opportunity.

In business, market up and down take place and in such situations you need to find right opportunities to make your business run smoothly. When you think on prospectus of diversification, even though there is business up-down, your product kitty makes sure to account sales to different client. You create opportunities, you prepare new product and sell it to new customers. Whenever you try a new approach, it is guaranteed that you will get ample opportunities of growth in this sector.

Learning is one field which gives you opportunities to prosper. When you add certain qualification, you increase your serviceability circle.
People know you by several credentials .This gives you scope to experiment in different area and because of

which your span, control and authority also increases.

Positive approach in dealing helps to receive new opportunities. For every new entrepreneur, the entry level is very very difficult if he is starting things on his own without any internal or external support. He has to struggle for his identity in market as well as he has to put large effort to make things workable. For new entrepreneur, the first break received involves either a difficult work which is avoided by others or a simple work in which there is very very less profit. Now it is your choice whether if you want to create your identity through difficult work or easy work. Accordingly you have to choose the right opportunity in front of your table and deliver your best. Once you create your name in the market, more people will enquire with you, negotiate with you for price and delivery and finally provide you order to fulfill. But the initial struggle is very very critical and you have to build your willpower to recognize the potential in opportunity and stay firm on its accomplishment.

There are two types of people in organization, one who allot you opportunity and one who constantly in search of opportunities. The people who allot opportunities are senior players in the game. They are always in search of right talent to collaborate and contribute to their missions. You have to recognize such leaders and you have to find out avenues through which you can build rapport with them. Introduction, general discussion, display of your key skills and achievement is all seen before allotting an opportunity.

The second types of people who always go for opportunities are people with high affinity to deliver their best. These people have pleasant personality, they gel easily with others, they ask lot of questions and hence able to get information about what is happening inside and outside office environment. Several times they openly share they are available for new project and they can be considered with review of their previous track record. Because of this networking capability, they get new work and their able team in the backyard fulfills the received orders. Here before committing to client, they assess the internal functioning, internal issues and try to commit based on prevailing situations. This mechanism is helpful for building trust with client and it help to provide more opportunities.

Initiative is important factor in recognizing opportunity. When the world is sleeping, you have to arise, plan your day and then take small and simple steps to fulfill your dream. Early rise is example of freshness, energy and positive spirit. When you approach with this attitude, the success is guaranteed!

Friends, the lost opportunities give resentment and limit your efforts for some time. In such cases , you have to keep trying hard, keep pushing hard till the right opportunity knock your door . Hear the knock and grab the opportunity.

Hope you like this chapter ! Let's pause here!

SKILL 161 : LEARNING THROUGH MISTAKE SKILL

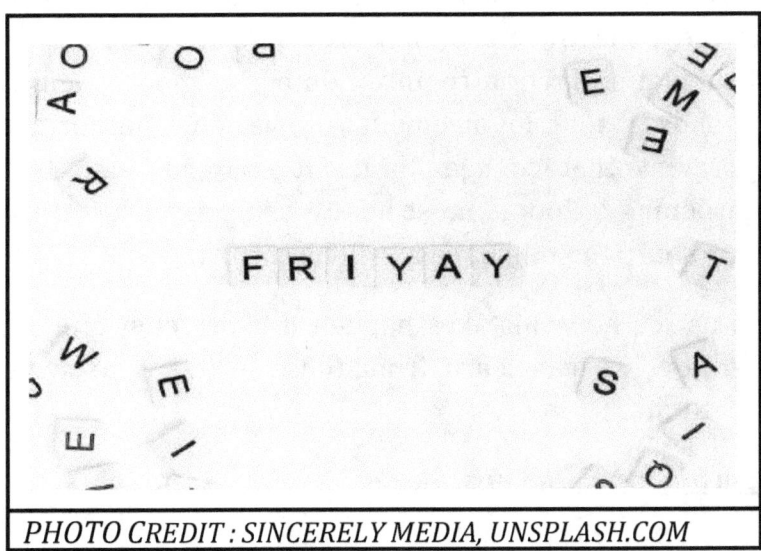

PHOTO CREDIT : SINCERELY MEDIA, UNSPLASH.COM

Dear Friends,

Good Evening and welcome to yet another skill chapter -Learning through mistake skill! Let's go into thedetails.

> " Mistakes happen unknowingly but they create major loss . Learning through mistake is expensive skill and hence efforts need to be done to learn thingsclearly before doing!"

THE SKILL ARCHITECT

When we are working in fast paced world, mistakes are bound to happen. When mistakes happen they create delay, defect and disadvantages. Rectification of mistakes is a big task and it requires changes in physical appearance as well as document correction. Sometimes, physical correction is easy and can be done in one or two day however sometimes document correction require number of months and it depends upon involvement of various authorities approving that change. Hence it is wisely said that sharpening of tool is must before using axe for cutting, more sharp the tool is, easy will be cutting.

Let us see how mistakes happen in work environment and how we can learn from these mistakes to avoid repetition.

Learning through mistakes:

- Error in material selection happens because of miss out in noting design specifications. Every product is designed and constructed for specific work environment. If the work environment is not studied properly, choice of effective material to suit that environment creates error and it cause selection of inappropriate material. To avoid the same, various standards and specification are derived and standardized. We need to refer these standards before finalizing material for typical service environment. Errors in material are costly and rectification at any stage is costlier as you have to work again with new material with relevant document correction.

- Error or mistake of design is major mistake and it affects complete batch and its associated product. Any design has two parts; one is drafting of part as per graphical views and second is a design calculation confirming strength of designed part. Error in design calculation will create weak parts and this part will not be able to withstand applicable loading. They will fail in service immediately or after some abrupt loading. Such errors are avoided by carrying out pilot run with given construction and studying part behavior under various loading condition. If required increasing strength of a member by either replacing material, increasing thickness or changing area. Error in representation has effect on geometry of part and if part is not fixed where it required, the total efforts will go in vain. Part correction requires redesign to applicable dimension and reconstruction according to new drawing. You have to check how many batch products are affected and hence you have to correct all those parts. Its major learning and all efforts need to done to block such errors in pilot product testing phase.

Mistake in part construction occurs because of incorrect reading of drawings. The design is correct, drafting is correct, material is also correct but during construction if dimensions are not referred correctly, the errors will happen. Such errors will be highlighted in assembly stage where misfit, mismatch or excessive gaps are created which reflects the seriousness of error. To avoid such errors, every drawing needs to be studied carefully before starting part construction .

- Document errors happen because of incorrect entries. Document error correct confusion in calculations, final amount, final weight, final quantity and it leads to mis understanding. Suppose by mistake the total bill is reduced by 1 lakhs for a supplied material, here supplier will have loss of 1 lakhs. Suppose on document 100 parts are supplied and physically 90 parts are received, the purchaser will be at loss of 10 parts and its price. Hence co-relation of physical items along with their bill of material is important in every buying and selling transaction. If same documentation is related with statutory authorities, we have to take their approval and there may be number of questions asked to find out and resolve reason of errors. With the help of latest software's, a detailed fact check can be ensured now days to find out any error in documentation.

Friends, to err is human. Errors happen from everyone and we have to learn from those errors. We have to ensure that error is corrected, communicated and avoided by others!

Hope you like this chapter. Let's pause here!

SKILL 162 : CAPACITY ENHANCEMENT SKILL

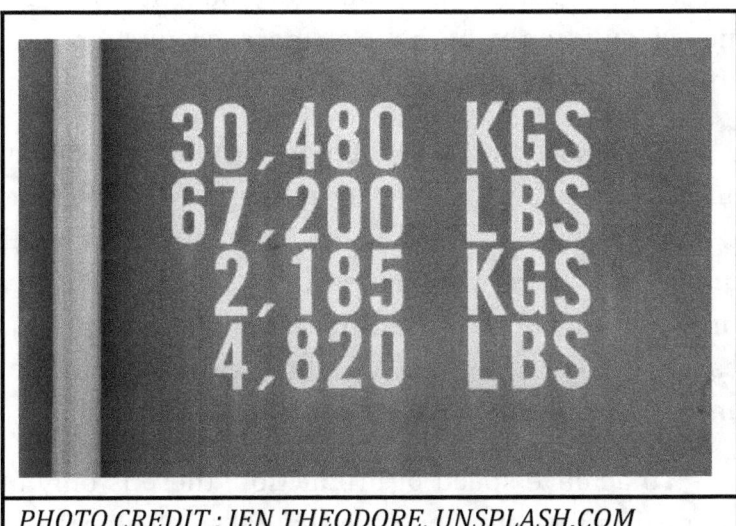

PHOTO CREDIT : JEN THEODORE, UNSPLASH.COM

Dear Friends,

Good Evening and welcome to yet another skill chapter – capacity enhancement skill! Let's go into the details!

> *"Capacity enhancement assures improved performance, progressive learning and completion of work before committed time. Capacity is increased by larger size of machines or longer working hours!"*

There are phases through which any organization grows. In initial few years, you struggle for orders and branding of your service and product. As you earn name & fame for your contribution, demand of your product increases several fold. This is a major opportunity to convert the demand into monetary benefits. But it is achieved only with the help of more production, quick production and instant supply.

To achieve the target of more production you have to increase number of people and associated machines. You can increase working hours by allowing minimum hours of overtime with increased wage rate. You can improve production by setting advanced machine and latest operating systems. By this entire means your chances of achieving more production are achieved.

To achieve speed of production, there is only one option – distribution of work in several small work packs and assembling at central location with ready to fit hardware and joining material. This activity require easy design which can be assembled and fixed in less time. If design has intricate shape and difficult assembly, this clause will not work. As the skill level increases same people in same time can do more work. This is possible because human brain support repeat activity easily. Once you set your hand with the process the neural network delivers to provide result. Quickness is also achieved by installing higher rpm machines with increased flow rate. Now the team working on such fast paced machine has to adopt fast processing approaches and they have to ensure

100% availability of required material before starting of machine.

For quick supply of these parts, supply capacity can be enhanced by adding effective network of distributors, dealers and authorized agents. These people contribute to supply scheme by directly or indirectly interacting with potential buyers. The time required for supply at customers gate is reduced by inventory stocking and providing the material in local area as soon as the order is received. To store such material you need big space and same is arranged by warehouse owner. The capacity of warehouse and his credit with manufacturer decides the optimum stocking level. We have seen many small suppliers purchase form such wholesale suppliers. This is because, if they want to purchase from factory, they have to order huge quantity. This is because, factory has number of overheads and to maintain profitability they require certain number of product to pass the break –even point. Hence wholesalers who purchase directly from company places required orders and get the required material. Down the line adding their commission they sell it to small supplier, through these supplier material reaches retail buyers. Now capacity of retail buyer is enhanced with the sales target they achieve as they serve for number of years. This is a task of patience and as their customer base increases their sales increases. The capacity of wholesaler increases as they add more facilities to assist supply. With huge purchase company offer a least possible per product price which keeps wholesalers margin intact .

Finally the capacity of factory is enhanced by adding more branches and integrating their operations through either central administration or by structuring several performance divisions to account individual centers performance separately. This also help to focus on putting additional efforts in area where there is less strength or less demand.

With increased capacity, problems also increases if your systems are not mature and proper training of workforce is not carried out. Handling such facilities become a day to day challenge and after some time people come to conclusion that system need to establish here. Actually system is nothing but standard way of doing operations , then there may be one part to be made or thousand , the operations, discipline and speed will remain equally same which will benefit to produce products with less errors and minimum delays . This discipline is must to ensure standard practice.

Many multinational organizations develop their branches with the help of core experienced team. This team has several experiences of building your brand in new place and their expertise is applied for such capacity expansion programmes. They take all care of creating first part from that facility and then they handover the facility to new team with constant review of their performance.

Hope you like this chapter! Let's pause here!

SKILL 163 : SPACE MANAGEMENT SKILL

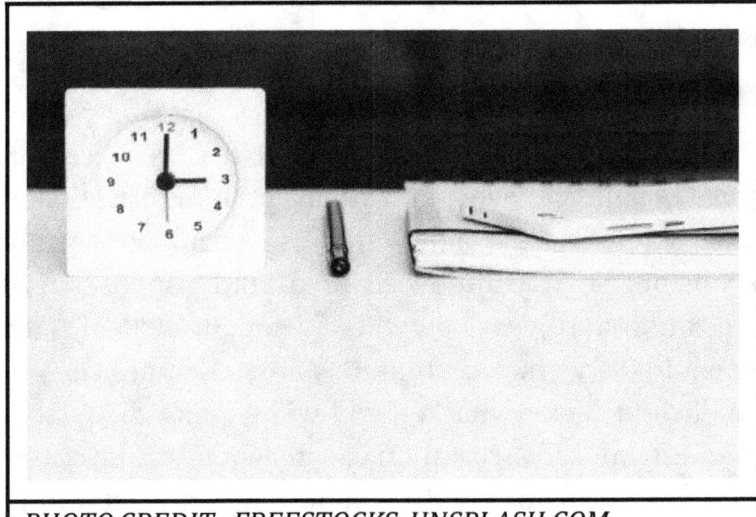

PHOTO CREDIT : FREESTOCKS, UNSPLASH.COM

Dear Friends,

Good morning and welcome to yet another skill chapter – Space management skill! Let's go into the details!

> *"Space management is about placing things in sequence and order to save time in handling, processing and dispatching. A streamline is necessary!"*

Friends, one of the most important aspects of fast operations of any factory is systematic implementation of its plant layout. Plant layout is absolute and exact placement of machines, storage area, passages for movement and office places, nearness to nearest port or transport station and generally central location for fast distribution to their customers. This layout planning is very much necessary to use floor space in most efficient way.

Strategic location of a firm decides its success in future business expansion. You invest in industrial land which is in acres and which is meant for future expansion. So if your purchase a land supposes 100 acres, in first 10 year you will develop 30-40% of same depending on your current business volume. As you establish in certain market, you will expand the facility by adding more workstations as per identical layout or different layouts. With adhering to statutory regulations, you have to develop the land according to best possible layout structure. In any industry there is clear cut sequence of entry of material, processing of material and then final dispatch of material. It is the idea of layout designer to ensure quick access to facility which is done by designing internal transportation with wide roads and quick entry to storage places. As soon as vehicle enters in the factory, you should be able to download the material and make its document to send it for further processing. If there is que of vehicles, then the multiple window system has to be planned to ensure quick movement. This is done with reference to prior knowledge of material movement frequency. Suppose in a day you are certain about in warding of 30 vehicles with every vehicle taking about an hour for unloading it is quite obvious that this load cannot be managed by single window, here you have to arrange for additional position to make things fast and easy.

Same thing is applicable for dispatch section. Every factory has a typical dispatch pattern. In some factories ,dispatches happens almost per minute while in some factories dispatches happen in certain fixed interval of month such as last week of every month. Such firms will produce their product in first three week and finally in the last week they will deliver to respective customers. Now in such a layout the roads should be designed in such a way that receipt and dispatch vehicle will not cross each other. When the material is in warded , it should have unique entry door and when the material is being dispatched the vehicle should enter from dispatch gate and should leave from same gate . This ensures accurate record keeping at every gate and at the end of the month or year , we can easily find out inward transaction and total dispatches accurately to tally with financial record. This is because the financial record in the form of GRN is generated at stores while the INVOICE is created at dispatch . When we work out total sales through invoice and subtract the total GRN entry , we get the manufacturing cost required for employment of manpower, machine operations, other overheads and daily production management.By keeping good control on this internal cost the profit percentage can be maintained.

Inside factory and their processing plant, the space management is done with the help of assembly sequence. There is material entry at workstation and for near place the material is stocked, when material passes stage one it is moved to subsequent stage in line or in parallel depending upon type of product being produced. For a line assembly, space is managed with serial layout. Till the completion of first operation, next operation cannot be started. Once set line production has advantage of fast movement and more production. In parallel layout management there are separate work centers and they are not dependent on each other output directly. It means if a work is being done at one work center it will get complete in one day while work at other center may take three day, during assembly the completed stages will be assembled and their output will be given to next work center. So here space management follow independent arrangement of work facility to ensure every work center do their work irrespective of other work center.

Location of several offices such as guest house, security cabin, canteen and pantries, recreation centers, playground, garden is important part of space management and due attention is given to ensure easiness and style in the design. The more spacious the open area, it will add to aesthetics of your facility which create first impression in the minds of your customer. Hope you like this chapter! Let's pause here!

SKILL 164 : DESIGNER SKILL

PHOTO CREDIT : KELLY SIKKEMA, UNSPLASH.COM

Dear Friends,

Good morning & welcome to yet another skill chapter – Designer skill! Let's go into the details!

> " Design has to be simple, safe, replicable , authentic, spacious and functional . Designer put their best possible efforts and experience to create practical designs!"

There are number of televisions present in the market, but a typical brand has more sales !

There are number of vehicle in the market but a typical model sells to great extent !

There are number of payment applications in your mobile web store ,however a typical application has maximum number of subscribers!

There are various social media sites and applications , however only particular brand has maximum subscribers !

Do you know the reason of success of these brands?

Its noting but an exceptionally user friendly design and at the same time robust internal construction which assures safety, performance and ease of operation .

Let's see point wise , how designers design their product .

Designer Approach :

- Every designer when start imagining their product , they have certain basic assumptions and principles . The size ,shape and soundness of product have prime importance which is followed by arrangement of supporting parts to carry out a desired function . The main processing unit always has a central mechanism which is run by allied & peripheral components . We have seen in the engineering that every part has typical role in its design and they deliver to provide result. To explain the same , let's see few examples. The design of mobile handset follows a rectangular shape just to ensure it fits in your pocket . Secondly the rectangular shape is relevant with standard notebook with which data can be read in traditional way . Design of a wheel is round just to ensure minimum contact area with the surface and to maintain the speed for which it is designed . In less energy the wheel get its moments because of dynamics of motion involved in its regular operation. Design of various key follow the identical match with its recess and easy fitting and removal . A key avoids relative movement of part and hence it is important to adhere recess geometry . We know there are number of key types such as taper key , counter sunk key . They serve the purpose to hold the part correctly.

Once basic size is determined , the second factor is supportive strength calculations and study of part under applicable loading condition . The parts generally loaded either in tension, compression, fatigue , torsional, etc. Based on their static and dynamic loading condition , designer arranges the stresses with respect to materials yield strength and ultimate tensile strength . Strength is proportionated with the help of changing material thickness . This factor sets the required strength and in all possible loading patterns the material will perform to its expected level.

- Aesthetics follows knowledge of advanced fashion and style statements which is upgraded regularly. We have seen with emergence of LED & LCD the traditional CRT panel of television got replaced by sleek LED screens . Which looks extremely and can be fitted in less space ? The earlier design of number of mobile handset is replaced by very very compact touch screen devices. Be it a Tab or Laptop or smartphone , the technological advances in display design has shown wonders for its users.

- User friendliness is important design parameter considered by designer . When we observe latest social communication system , they have combined the general social decisions to make it easy to record your response . These options are easily understandable and lot of people finds it easy to use . Suppose we are carrying out an online transaction , the payee and beneficiary details along with bank code and amount supported by OTP and password do your work with instant messaging at both ends. This is nothing but user friendliness aspect in design consideration .

- A successful design has simplicity, cost effectiveness and wide scale production capability .

Hope you like this chapter! Let's pause here! ✍

SKILL 165 : NEATNESS SKILL

PHOTO CREDIT : MATTHEW T RADER,

Dear Friends,

Good Afternoon and welcome to yet another skill chapter- Neatness skill . Let's go into the details.

> *" Neatness at work or home keep things in order and accessible. Its highly personal skill and it represent the general awareness about surrounding atmosphere!"*

Neatness, it may be in office or in home, create wonders. It is prerequisite of a successful person. If you study the daily habit of any successful people, you will observe they either do things clearly and neatly or they employ people who can do the things neatly. Neatness creates a lasting impression. It is the best and simple way to present your work to others. When people find the shown work is neat and clean, they review it in detail and when the content is liked they appreciate. Let's see ,point wise the neatness habits at work and home.

Neatness at work & home :

- For office in a standardized layout, you have allotted a standard workspace. Here you can keep your files and folder in easily visible pattern. You can arrange them in month wise upgrade or you can keep them into separate compartment and labeling the compartment for easy accessibility.
- The general stationary which includes pen, pencil, notebook, stapler, punching machine, calculator, and note pads has to be arranged systematically and whenever you wish to access it, it should be accessible.

Files stored in computer have to give right titles so that they can be easily identified and forwarded wherever required. A false title to created content increases confusion and because of which correct file is not found. Hence the exact sequence of drive- folder- file – file name- file type has to be followed.

- Now a days, so many file formats are available based on medium in which we wish to transfer the data electronically. This has references like pdf, doc, docs, png, gif, epub. Accordingly you have to carry out conversions. A well formatted file reach safely at desired destination and hence make your work simple.
- Neatness of reporting is important to communicate the status clearly. In digital reporting, the essential details of unit, its customer references, the time frame in which part is made, stage details and your observations and supporting photographs provide clear idea to its reader. Such reports are shared in various meeting to present the facts and take decisions. Hence such reports need to be neat, clean and simple.
- Neatness of purchase order requires detailed clarity of terms and conditions of supply. The ordered quantity, its unit price and tax liability. Any change in detailing affect the supply adversely. Hence this document needs to be clear and easily readable. Its good habit to correct purchase order terms before the part is manufactured or sold out.

    Neatness of process is observed in remark free audits. An audit reviews your processes as per set guidelines and observes if there are any differences. When you receive the remark free audit report it is the result of neatness in your process and their maintenance.
- Neatness at home is seen with proper arrangement of your room, your regular accessories, your personal folder filing, and the general cleanliness in your day to day activities. Number of personal habits of neatness

projects your inclination to carry out your work with accuracy and completeness. When you practice neatness, the interest required to carry out work remains same. If the things are not neat and dirty, naturally the interest level drops and it create error in your work.

- The impact of neat work is seen in the form of appreciation of work from clients, statutory officials and guest visiting your facility. When such guest visits different places they share same experience with others as ideal example of neatness.
- Neatness is also responsible to maintain hygiene at workplace & at home. When you see a fully packed hospital which is cleaned every alternative hour, the cleanliness is simple commendable. When you see a house neat and open, you suddenly feel fresh and your mood become happy. These are basic things but these things account to huge level when we want to achieve success in our life.

Friends, hope you like this chapter. Neatness is a good habit, always cherish it!

Let's pause here!

SKILL 166 : ACCURACY BUILDING SKILL

PHOTO CREDIT : HANS RENIERS, UNSPLASH.COM

Dear Friends,

Good afternoon and welcome to yet another skill chapter- Accuracy building skill! Let's go into the details!

> *" Accuracy depends of collection of details, sincerity of efforts and exact knowledge of things . Rest is completion in sequence and order !"*

The competitive workspaces thrive to achieve excellence in their everyday operations. They build systems and develop people to deliver best results. The accuracy of their product is based on accuracy of its design, the exactness of its construction and to the point installation to connect with allied systems and start performing . Let us see point wise how accuracy is built up in the system .

Accuracy Building in system:

• An accurate workplace always has mix of qualified & experienced people of all ages. This team continuously evaluates their own work before presenting to others. This is the basic reason why they achieve success in their operations. The self-evaluation process highlights minute errors and timely removal of these errors makes your work accurate and presentable.

• Accuracy of product design is supported by product strength calculations. Engineering is a clear science . For every engineering product there is fix and certain formula for occurrence of particular event or action . The laws of physics and mathematical equations govern the general mechanism of every engineering part assembly. In a professional work place , people have clear foundation which makes them design correct things in accurate manner .

• Experience of past errors also increases accuracy in next level . With past experience you get idea about how things go wrong . Next time you block those errors .

The corrected portion of the part is carefully observed for its details. On satisfactory observation we can say that the part is correct.

- Study of tolerances is main thing to achieve desired accuracy level. When you are working with wider tolerance, let's say dimensional tolerance within 'mm ', you can achieve the same with manual processes or semi-automatic processes. However when you have to achieve tolerance within microns, you have to use CNC machines with desired accuracy level. Hence tolerance governs your accuracy. You require dimension 100 mm within 0.1 plus or minus tolerance, then any reading between 99.9 to 100.1 is acceptable. This range of dimension is going to fit with matching part. However anything in excess of 100.1 or less than 99.9 will not serve its purpose and even for fraction of 0.01 mm, the dimension will not be accurate. Hence understanding of tolerance is much more important.

People work for years to achieve desired accuracy. In a typical casting industry, obtaining a defect free casting is always a big task. In first two or three trials even after setting correct parameters, you encounter minor issues. When you fine tune parameters, you achieve success. Casting being intermediate or final process, surface of cast part can be as cast or machined. For as cast parts the tolerance level is generally higher. Whereas for machined casting the tolerance level is stringent. This way accuracy of same part differs with respect to its surface condition in final assembly.

- Small improvement projects done to improve

process sequence, additional care and control on variations also increases accuracy . With every small improvement we come near to desired dimension . The development of fine grained steel follows such sequence of multiple experiments in melting cycles . Steel made at various melting temperature range and different composition provide accurate result of mechanical properties . When your part meets the property requirement accurately in destructive test it is nothing but the result of accurate composition set up within applicable range, maintaining the heat cast details in same element range and uniform solidification throughout its cross section . The accuracy of each stage decides the final property achievement of given steel.

- Accuracy of software depends on the accuracy of programmes, building logic and electronic part assembly . The structure of integrated circuits makes the computation possible which follow a digital logic .

Hope you like this chapter. Let's pause here!

SKILL 167 : ERROR SENSING SKILL

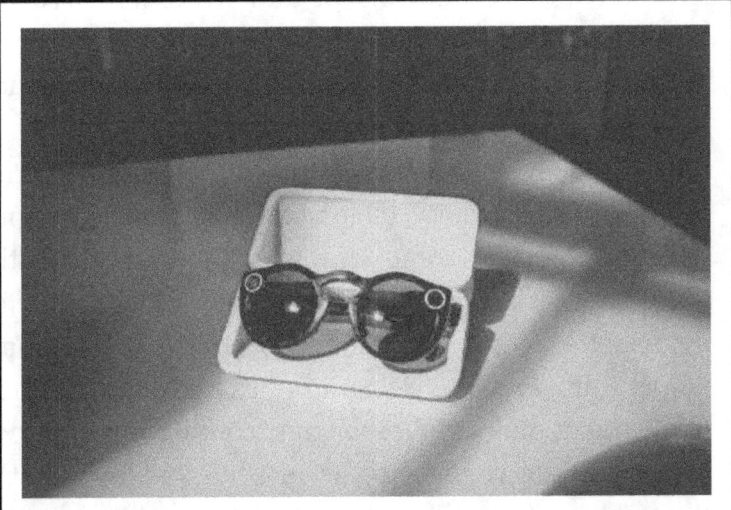

PHOTO CREDIT : NEONBRAND, UNSPLASH.COM

Dear Friends,

Good Evening and welcome to yet another skill chapter- Error sensing skill . Let's go into the details.

> *" Error sensing is first step to improve accuracy . When you sense possible chances of errors , you avoid it and hence prepare accurate parts. Error sensing requires thoughtful study and hand on experience !"*

- A set up was offered for inspection in a factory. The inspector was experienced. When he came near the job, he found out inappropriate orientation of part. Being regular with this design the inspector is aware about its construction details. When they checked the part in detail, their observation found true. The part wad mis fit and which is corrected after inspector's remark. People agreed their error and promised to correct next set up with clear study of drawing before proceeding further.
- For a seasoned cashier getting feel of the currency note is quite a daily task. Many instances happen where depositor comes to deposit the money in the bank or withdraw the money in bank and during transaction, sometimes one or two notes remain short or excess. Seasoned cashier with their experience guess the error and count the notes two times before registering it in their ledger. In the instance of duplicate note, they immediately observed the difference in feel of surface and intimate accordingly to their respective authority. This alertness and error sensing is what expected from seasoned cashier.
- In a process layout, every part is fitted in sequence but exit path is left open and arrangement is not done to keep exit path below ground. An experienced engineer raises their concern on same and convinces the team regarding recent advancement in fluid discharge and same need to left underground. The team checks the details and accept their error and correct the things before

they layout is implemented in practice. This engineer is regular subscriber of statutory body releasing recent development in his field of interest. This keeps him aware and updated about latest happenings in his domain. This habit has saved considerable cost related to project layout.

- In a typical valve assembly the direction of valve and accessories was reversed. A new workman noted this error. He reviewed drawing and checked the orientation. He found out there is error in assembly. He immediately notified to respective supervisor and before carrying out test with assembly they corrected the valve orientation. If this had missed, there may be operational problem during test and the part could have damaged. A keen eye to details sensed this error early and avoided major damage.

In engineering drawing the bill of material and part details are drafted correctly. However few quantities are not entered correctly. An experienced production manager senses it early and highlight with design department. The respective design engineer checks it and accepts his error in counting and overlooking the detailed arrangement. The drawing is corrected and bill of material is updated before material is procured. If this error had noted after material procurement, for additional material shop people may have to wait for more time which could have increased idle time and it could have pressure of final dispatch date because of intermittent unnecessary delay. This delay is avoided by error sensing skill .

- When we read 100 books, we can write our own book . When we carry out work 100 times , we can design its next model . When we encounter with hundred hurdles , we find out our own way of passing through its difficulty levels. When we do difficult things again & again , we build confidence to deal with them and finally we achieve our goals . Error sensing skill require hard work in the field, experience of working with adversities, experience of working in number of shits and work location , this is because people changes with location , their attitude changes with shifts and many errors are occurred only because of lack of complete attention . Daily touch with your work makes things easy to understand and implement . In daily work, we discuss things with colleagues and with such sharing our knowledge increases. Next time when we see similar error , we get alert and correct the things instantly . This is all required before sensing error . As per popular saying, a stitch in time saves nine . An error sensed in right time avoids major rework andmajor part damage .

Hope you like this chapter. Let's pause here!

SKILL 168 : MULTIPLE CONCEPT APPLICATION SKILL

PHOTO CREDIT : SHAREGRID, UNSPLASH.COM

Dear Friends,

Good Morning & Welcome to yet another skill chapter- Multiple concept application skill. Let's go into the details.

> "Simple problems has simple approach, difficult problems require application of multiple concept and their effective implementation to come out of crisis. "

In a complex work environment, lots of activities happen same time. People are occupied with various targets and in achieving same priorities are set out. Number of times these priorities are met and fulfilled but sometimes because some milestones are missed, the subsequent operations pile up and this gives rise to creation of mess, sometimes big mess.

Resolution of complexities at work requires thoughtful action plan and logical communication. Let's look with the help of few practical situations how the complex issues are handled.

Multiple concept application in complex situations:

- What will you do if you note failure of part while testing and retesting?
  The obvious decision is rejection by inspecting authority but when you have given the task to find out what are the reasons of failure, it becomes necessary to go into step by step details and application of multiple concepts for this rejection. First thing you find out part drawing and its design calculations. You check every aspect that contributes to strength of part. When you find out there is no issue with designcalculation, you move to construction sequence. In construction sequence first we check material test certificates supplied by mills and their in- house testing result once receiving in premises as a part of cross checking procedure. It is standard practice that if there is

considerable variation in properties, the differences will be highlighted at that stage only. When you find out material is okay and design is okay, you move to check its way of construction in the form of real orientation and dimensional accuracy. Whether parts are fitted at actual distance or not. Change in dimension affects the internal stresses. When a part deals with external and internal environment, the stresses are balanced in equitable proportion. If the dimensions are not maintained as per applicable stress pattern, there is change in these stress patterns which disturbs the state of uniform loading hence structural stability in static and dynamic loading condition. So, the reason of failure can be dimensional or orientation misses out. Now if you find that this concept is also okay, you find it surprising to locate root cause. Because everything is clear and still error is happening. Now it is final checkpoint to see whether the test apparatus is correct. To find out this reason you remove test piece from failed part and test it at other laboratory. You provide testing standard, test specimen and observe the result. Now to your surprise, the part found out correct. With this result you open your test apparatus and its calibration status. During internal inspection you find out that there are malfunctioning of certain sensors and their allied systems which is causing trouble in testing above certain temperature or above certain stress, below that level the apparatus is working fine and hence you never encountered any issue. With this observation, you go on repairing and recalibrating your test apparatus and then retest the part with new test specimen from same part.

This part shows exact result which is shown in external lab. Both results match and now you are fully assured of the root cause.

You take up the matter with inspecting agency and request them to come again for retest. You put forward complete details of failure in test and subsequent actions done by you to find out the root cause. Before witnessing test, authorities review your documents and after satisfactory conclusion, they agree to witness the test.

During witness they ensure every sensor is working clearly and observations are recorded properly. The test is carried out to complete satisfaction and required results are achieved. The customer also notes the result and they accept the material without any remark.

The documentation is done with attachment of all test details and necessary approval link. This way with the help of multiple concept application the live & practical concern of inappropriate failure is resolved. Every difficult problem can be solved with its systematic analysis.

Hope you like this chapter. Let's pause here! ✍

SKILL 169 : FUNDAMENTAL KNOWLEDGE SKILL

PHOTO CREDIT : TONI ZATT, UNSPLASH.COM

Dear Friends,

Good afternoon and welcome to yet another skill chapter – Fundamental knowledge skill. Let's go into the details.

> *"Fundamental knowledge is critical to link current knowledge. When you are dealing with new concepts, you must know the soul of that concept which isfundamental knowledge!"*

Friends, scientific study is about observation of natural principles and setting mathematical relationship with variables observed. In academics, more focus is given to express the rules of nature in conjunction with science behind it. This science help you find out happening of events with a cause behind it. This empirical study has accounted stream of fundamental sciences which deals with branches of science in the form of physics, chemistry and mathematics. Let it be laws of motion, laws of thermodynamics, laws of mass transfer, laws of conservation of energy or any chemical reaction involving phases and oxidation, reduction, neutralization mechanism, the basic equation remains same and which is based on relationship within variables.

In any interview when questions are asked about explaining a concept, the successful candidate always explains his knowledge with supporting examples. The examples are based on scientific principles and he write down all necessary formulae which show the grip on the subject. Let it be any question, he answer them quickly because his foundation is strong. Suppose a candidate is asked to explain the principles of welding and various arc welding process in his engineering interview, he has to convey answers with proper definition of welding, the importance of heat and pressure in welding process, the characteristic of material to be joined, its phase equilibrium diagram, the melting point of material and hence its heat dissipation capacity, setting of electrical current to melt the material easily. The qualification of process and qualification of people before starting welding. The best process for welding given material and next best process as second option. The kind of defects observed in process and how they can be rectified. The testing methods to assess the strength of the welding and hence the codes governing the test. The quantity of raw material and welding consumable required before welding and the ways of waste reduction. The heat treatment knowledge and knowledge about various temperature control and furnace environment understanding. The identification and traceability of welded structure and its documentation.

When you answer all these questions correctly, your knowledge is appreciated. So when you are given a new assignment, it is very very easy to deal with challenges as they occur. Let's check with few examples. Suppose during welding ,lot of spatters are occurred , you will check current setting , gas mixture ration and ways with which welding torch to work piece distance is controlled . When you give necessary instructions to your team and observe the performance, your problem gets resolved. Suppose the welding is forming cracks. You will immediately look at electrode moisture & electrode baking temperature, then you will see material preheat requirement and also observe is there any major restraint in set up which is causing stress concentration, secondly you will see post heating and post weld heat treatment compliance, interpass cleaning and temperature, you will also see the cooling rate and if there is thermal gradient which is causing sudden cracking tendency. You will act on these points and will make your welding crack free.

There are proficiency levels of welding expertise. As a welding expert you must aware about choice of right electrode to weld given material, up to how much thickness you can weld with given process, the heat input requirement and the process capability . With more expertise, the fundamental knowledge becomes easy to handle. As you spend lots of time of your career with same process, you began to find the actual practical case studies and how the mechanism work to resolve the issues occurred.

It is the power of knowledge which let you correct the wrong thing by carrying out repair and replacement. The strength of fundamental knowledge is that it suddenly suggests you the shortest way out because you are aware of all ways. Where a novice can struggle to find way out, experienced person will find its remedy by using fundamental knowledge and different tricks he followed in his career journey. Knowledge is constant and we have to add knowledge as we progress in life. The more updated we are about latest happenings, more comfortable we are with changes proposed. When we improve our ability to cope up with changes, difficulties get converted into solutions. Hope you like this chapter. Let's pause here!

SKILL 170 : DIRECTION BUILDING SKILL

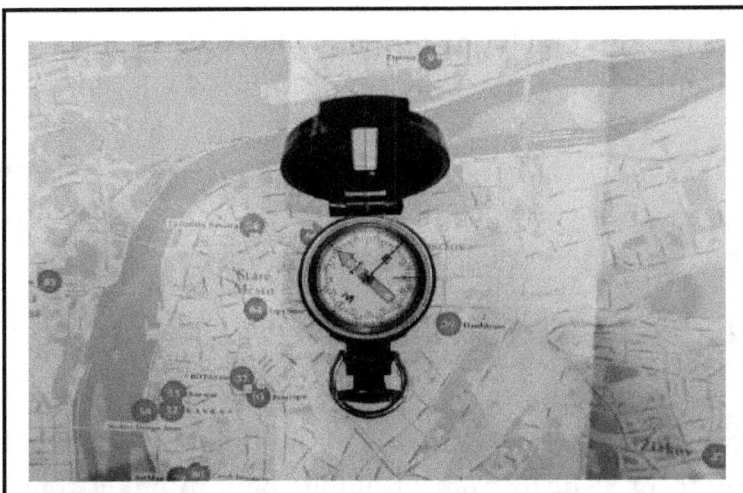

PHOTO CREDIT : DENISE JANS, UNSPLASH.COM

Dear Friends,

Good afternoon and welcome to yet another skill chapter- direction building skill! Let's see this skill in detail!

> " *Directions guides decisions. A right direction make the path of success visible while a wrong direction make the success path difficult !*"

THE SKILL ARCHITECT

Friends, as far as life is concerned, the importance of right direction is very much vital. At various phases we are blessed with people who direct us to fetch our path of success. Be it parent, teachers, seniors, authorities we always guided for right direction. When we became mature enough to understand the situations and our response to those situations, we direct ourselves. This is the phase in our life where we take our own decision and either enjoy its benefits or suffer its losses. The whole idea of direction building skill is to make you strong enough to handle crisis situation and come out of it as a strong winner. Let's us see point wise, how direction building skill is acquired.

Direction Building Skill Acquisition:

- In academic life , directions are important to know more about how to do study , how to learn practical's, how to present in front of public, how to enjoy sports and how to gel with friends. This is part of our upbringing. The environment around us determines our choices and behaviors.
- In college life, direction building is done for selection of right career path. Up to tenth everyone has same subjects but when we enter into college we see the available option to follow our career aspirations. The inclination, talent and opportunities decide the choice of right career. If you are good with mathematics and drawing, you opt for engineering. If you have excellent hold on science and especially biology along with affinity for society in which we live, we

select medical and prepare for hardest study our of all educational disciplines available. If we are excellent at accounting and we like to deal with cash , we select commerce while if we like to express our thoughts in the form of a picture, painting , song or a book , we opt for art . Lots of people having interest in leadership skills chose politics while those having interest in national service choose various military services. Our childhood, our upbringing and our talent influence us to choose a right career path. This is one of the major milestone of our life and selection of right direction decided your future success. Hence it is advisable to choose this option very very carefully & with confidence!

Once we enter career path, the directions are given by our seniors who have already in the middle of the journey and aware about the challenges in path. Building of a strong character is what expected from a successful career. On this path you not only learn technical factors of your work but you also learn how to behave with people around you to make yourself successful. After initial training when you develop yourself as executive with increasing span of responsibilities, your authority also increases. Here you make big decisions with discussions and guidance with your seniors. A phase is reached in career where you have to direct your team members. In this phase also, you use your earlier experience of dealing with challenges andcome out of it! There is system of Mentor & his disciple! This traditional approach has made

wonders in developing ones career.
- The false direction make you mature about how to handle failure. The path of failure is full of criticism, difficulties, uncomfortable moments and they test your stamina, perseverance, patience and above all your courage to deal with uncertainties and expectations. Here very people can guide you, most of the people will not pay attention to your status and they will wait quietly for your easy escape. Few near buddies will support and help you but you have to avoid this help and make sure you achieve your goals on your own efforts. This particular phase of direction building is very very tough and you have to maintain your cool throughout the stiff journey.
- At the end of every day, you have to review quietly whether I have done everything right? Will it create positive impact in people's life? Will it be beneficial for society? Will I get monetary benefits which I deserve? Will I receive the recognition for my work and efforts? The affirmative answers of these questions assure you that you are on right direction. These answers are the true indicators of path of direction building. Once you build it, all it requires to follow the path with your team.

Hope you like this chapter! Let's pause here!

SKILL 171 : APPROACH BUILDING SKILL

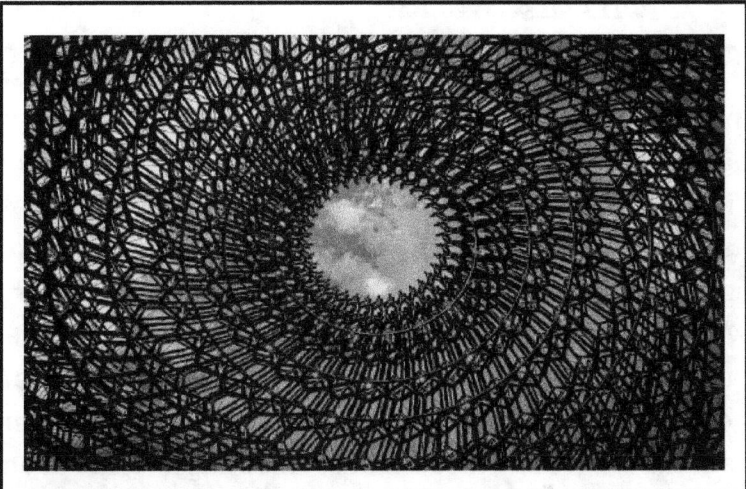

PHOTO CREDIT : TOM PODMORE , UNSPLASH.COM

Dear Friends,

Good afternoon and welcome to yet another skill chapter- approach building skill! Let's go into the details!

> " Approach make things easy or difficult . You can have participative approach , independent approach, investigative approach or reluctant approach ! Approach decide your stands!"

Friends, approach is fundamental identity of our decision making capability. Various situations occur in which we have to respond with right decision. Let's see with few practical examples which approach is to be used for specific situation .

Approach & Actions:

- **Participative approach:** This approach is used in team discussion. In this approach, within a team you have to discuss subject matter in detail and put your views on subject matter. This is most democratic method of working together. Here you can have agreement or differences but cumulatively majority wins the discussion with attachment of righteousness factor. The individual responsibility is limited and hence equal sharing of responsibility is important. Seminars, group discussions, meetings and events follow this approach.
- **Independent Approach:** In this approach, you have given a responsibility and you have to deliver results. Here right from scratch, you have to arrange things and at every step you have to check your progress. You may face challenges, certain difficulties but with the help of your knowledge, skill and experience you overcome it. Independent approach is observed is certain unique responsibilities such as carrying out tests, certifying person for their skill test, carrying out individual work pack of producing different part. Here the work is limited and execution is completely in your own hand. More efforts you put more are the benefits.

Some lucrative job titles such as actor, singer, and music director work in independent way to deliver results.

- **Investigative Approach:** Investigative approach is used to detect something and analyze its consequences. In this approach the parties involved are interrogated with several questions and the information is sought out. The information received is cross checked with factual evidences. When things found true, appropriate decisions are taken. Investigative approach is mostly used by manager to review the progress of their project and the work done by their team. Every team member has to answer correctly to present the status report. Particularly when customer complaints arrives, this approach is used to fix the root cause of complaints and accordingly responsibilities are allocated to specific individuals to fulfill.

- **Reluctant Approach:** Reluctant approach is used again by people who don't want to do allocated work. This approach is used to resist the change and maintain the status quo. The real skill of every leader is to identify such people in their team and motivate them to do good work. Reluctant people will find reason for everything and by any way they will show their incapability to carry out given operations. The gap between required knowledge and the skill of dealing with reluctance is important step in handling such people. You have to show & demonstrate the possible way with which work can be done. You have to stay with them for some time till that work is completed. In front of complete team, you have to show the path of making things happen. This approach blocks major reluctance in your field and make your environment a busy one &active one!

- Approach building according to situation increases your flexibility. Your approaches need to be mature and you should have well thought out till the last minute about different consequences of that approaches. Your potential to resolve problems is dependent of the choice of your approaches. A simple problems with wrong approach create issues while a difficult problem with right approach resolve the matters. Many times when you resolve the problems with fact based approach, your reputation as problem solver increases and this help you to establish as a leader. Whatever approach you take, you have to take into consideration, the total effect on cost, manpower and time. Your every effort should direct towards maximum benefit & saving of these resources. In fact approaches are taken for ultimate gain out of different business processes to stay in the game for long time!

Hope you like this chapter! Let's pause here!

SKILL 172 : OPTION MAKING SKILL

PHOTO CREDIT : ALEVISION , UNSPLASH.COM

Dear Friends,

Good Evening and welcome to yet another skill chapter – Option making skill! Let's go into the details!

> *" Options shows alternate ways to do work ! They offer flexibility of choice and increase level of freedom which make work easy and comfortable!"*

Friends, options are important part of decision making process. Management decisions follow a definite option availability process. When you are choosing a candidate for a specific role the first thing in front of hiring manager is the current status of work area and kind of performance and experience level required to deal with the situation . When interviews are carried out for the available role with several candidate the final shortlisting in the interview is done on the basis of overall track record, qualification, experience, challenges handled earlier, team handled earlier, package from previous employers and notice period with which candidate can join the organization in case of selection. Based on these factors, two or three candidates are selected for final round. In final round expected package and joining period is decided. The hiring manger has a certain allocate position budget plus surplus amount for right candidate. Negotiations happen with salary and finally the best candidate from available options is selected. Suppose in case the selected candidate don't join the organization and instead he stays with his previous organization with increased package, the management has to ask for second best candidate and work out his salary expectations and joining time. Now by this negotiation, management readily pays extra amount for which he was not selected at first instance or pay for his notice period for which earlier negotiation was stuck. With making a right offer, they select the candidate and provide them time for joining. This candidate joins the organization and process completes here. In case the candidate leaves the organization within probation period, a third option is contacted or a separate hiring process is conducted to choose right people for right job. For this reason recruitments are done with detailed care and confidential approach. Here the skill of hiring manager and network of recruiting manager act as impacting element in setting right options.

   Selection of correct supplier also follows same option making skill. You raise queries for material and receives quotations. You compare the quotation on technical and commercial aspects and offer purchase order to most favorable supplier after due negotiation. In negotiation, if a particular supplier doesn't agree to your commercial terms you discuss with other supplier till you get a favorable offer. In all these transactions you have to maintain the standard material procurement schedule. You have to take care of shop requirement and supplier negotiation. It should not happen that in between negotiations you are keeping your production house under long waiting. This increases pressure to perform and make things urgent at last minute. Hence material buyer has to finalize two or three optional supplier and has to set fix time interval to make buying decision. He has to use his communication skill, detailed market information, current market rate of various items and hence he has to offer the best possible rate for quick delivery. If one supplier doesn't agree, he has to procure from second options and thus make buying process easy and practical.

Many times we have to take decision on launch of product and its right time. Option making skill in this case act as major influencer. You can launch the part in certain territory where you have sound customer base. You can also have nationwide launch same time or international launch in same month. This helps you to sell fast and boost your customers. To fulfill the demand, you have to ensure, you have fulfilled production capacity and within determined time limit you can dispatch those product to your customer.

The variation in size and its price can act as major option making in selling consumer product. Every customer has different requirement. When product is designed, designer has to consider the requirement of class & budget of customer. So you will design a house as per 3 rooms' requirement, 4 room's requirement and 5 room's requirement. Accordingly your price will change and hence type of customers will change. If you want to deal with premium customers, you have to incorporate the best in class practices in your project that will appeal them to buy in great society. When you are designing for affordable range, you have to maintain a balance between your project cost, profit margin and amenities. This notion of making right options is important and act as indicator before making a purchase decision.

Hope you like this chapter! Let's pause here!

SKILL 173 : TECHNICAL SOUNDNESS SKILL

PHOTO CREDIT : BYRON STERK , UNSPLASH.COM

Dear Friends,

Good morning and welcome to yet another skill chapter -technical soundness skill! Let's go into the details!

> *"Technical soundness is about in depth technical awareness which involves benefits and disadvantages of a particular appliance, equipment or machine!"*

Friends, in a typical technological world, day to day progress happens and every new invention adds to different knowledge base to its users. Technical soundness skill is the knowledge required to handle technology easily. When you use technology for your day to day functions you increase your efficiency and make more time available to carry out your other aspirations.

Let's see point wise the importance of technical soundness:

Technical Soundness skill building:

1. Understand the principle of operation of any machine, equipment or appliance. Principle is basic thing on which the whole function is dependent. Around the central principle the parts are connected with each other by number of joining process. You need to have understanding of these processes also to note down the strength of every part. Once structure is known the rest is interaction of equipment with medium to derive process result. E.g. in a casting process when you pour metal (medium) into mold (machine) you find out the solidified metal with shape of the mold recess. When you draw the wire through number of dies, you get wires of various diameters. The principle used in casting involves melting of metal and putting in not stick mold. What will happen if metal get stick with mold, you will not able to get the desired shape. So this shape is achieved through coating inside mold which help to remove solidified metal from mold. In wire drawing control on diameter size is important. Force required to draw the wire is critical in this aspect. In powder metallurgy various shapes are prepared by making fine powder of material and then compacting, sintering the shape. The heat required to form bonds of particles is important and based on setting of these parameters, the overall strength of product is dependent. For a welded assembly the joint strength governs the long term performance of the part. Since the weld is supposed to have more strength than parent metal, number of assemblies is produced with welding and by following different welding practices. In a forged part the force of hammer decides the shape of the part. The die and its internal recess is important aspect to consider. Compare to casting, the forging has great strength but has limitation of manufacturing simple parts. Parts with intricate design details cannot be formed with forging. So this type of technical soundness is important while using technical products.

Be it civil stream , electrical stream or mechanical stream , every engineering part follow the logic of design principle – material of construction – central processing – manufacturing – completion and handing over or sales- installation – usage for defined purpose So instruction manual and in today world various product information videos give us an idea about the technical knowledge of these equipment. In carrying out domestic repairs of part, if you have tools and tackles then only it is advisable. If you don't have it, you should approach respective technician and authorized servicing center. Often demos are given to. make you aware about function of the part, but still if there is doubt about basic operation, you can take help of qualified person in the initial phase.

2. Every new technology offers added advantages and because of which the old one get replaced. Hence to keep our self-updated, a regular visit to tech inventions is necessary.

3. Newspapers, magazines and web portal provide ample information about the latest happenings in tech world along with experiments going on in the field. You must know the basic pattern and track record of such happenings. E.g. development of smartphones and electric vehicles is new buzz now days. Day to day new features is added in smartphone and it is becoming affordable also. Electric vehicles are creating interest about less emission, fuel efficiency, and pollution free environment. If we keep track of changes happening in this segment, we can build our technical soundness.

Hope you like this chapter! Let's pause here!

SKILL 174 : EXPERIMENTATION SKILL

PHOTO CREDIT : DIANA POLEKHINA, UNSPLASH.COM

Dear Friends,

Good morning and welcome to yet another skill chapter -Experimentation skill. Let's go into the details.

> *"Experiments give different results, sometime successful, sometimes failed one. But experiments set proof for success & failure!"*

The field of science is deeply related to study of natural principles for benefit of human. Principles, procedure, material required for experiments, observations, mathematical relationship and calculations, result of experiment and finally conclusion is the general way of carrying out experiments.

In practical work environment, to make changes successful, we have to carry out different experiments. Let's see different types of experiments carried out in practical environment.

- **_Technical Experiments:_**

They are done to evaluate the relation between technical variables. In achieving desired quality of product of process is optimized with setting of right parameters. Suppose you are carrying out residential complex internal development. You will try different combinations of colour themes, furniture and sofas, the variety of tiles and sanitary fitting. When all things are developed into sophisticated interior design it gives us the feel of a descent house. Here experimentation is done with aesthetics, colour scheme and design of interiors.

Another example of technical experiment is change of welding process to assess the feasibility of increased throughput. The speed of the welding is highly dependent of the process which is being used. When a certain metal is not easily weld able with one process, we change process to achieve desired results. Welding experiments can happen over size of the welding electrode, typical gas mixture, electrical characteristics, and the welding positions. Based on this study the optimum results are achieved.

- ***Financial Experiments:***

Financial experiments are done to control expenses and to reduce costs. The different financial structure of business function has different liabilities. Financial experiments are done to improve productivity and reduce liabilities. When you want to improve productivity, you have to motivate people by achieving various performance based opportunities. Wages as per enhanced productivity, bonus, increments, incentives, scholarships, financial awards are all means of financial experiment done to ensure competitiveness in the business. The result of this financial experiment can be complementary as well as challenging. Suppose a scheme become extremely successful, the financial experiment will be recorded and will be deployed in every part of the organization. If the scheme is failed and caused major loss, people will not follow this route in future. The risk associated with financial experiment is duly calculated before its implementation. If the risk is not analyzed properly, the quantum of loss could be several times. Before carrying out any financial experiment due care and approvals are necessary because the impact is huge on business.

- ***Human Experiment:***

Human experiment is carried out at workplace to implement various policy changes. Development of broad scale attitude change requires implementation of

Human resource strategies that will increase human participation, collaborative spirit and teamwork to make things happen. Inspiration, motivation. Mentoring, coaching, guidance is way of performing human experiment. In surveys and studies, a common opinion is formed by asking multiple questions or by allotting predetermined task to observe the results. Based on this result, the direction of further experimentation is decided. Suppose if you want to study how team behaves under pressure, you may carry out an aptitude test which will have challenging situations. You will record the answers of all questions for whole group and decide the common group opinion and their response to various situations. The response is further modified to suggest desired change and hence inculcating the ability to face challenges in actual life by using principles of coaching.

The experimentation ability broadens our thinking and makes us dare for right things. Whatever be the result, the experiment keeps us active and busy.

Hope you like this chapter. Let's pause here!

SKILL 175 : CONCLUSION SKILL

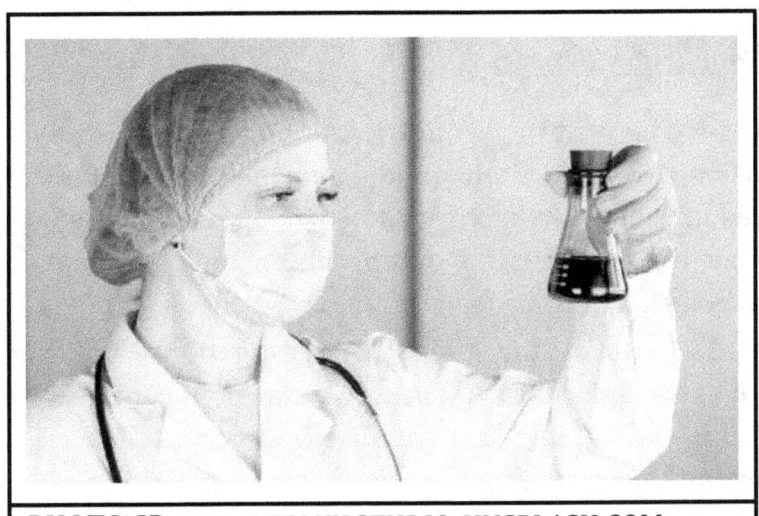

PHOTO CREDIT : BERMIX STUDIO, UNSPLASH.COM

Dear Friends,

> *" Conclusions are end results! They direct us to finish the things and move ahead towards new topic. When conclusion is correct, the whole story is reliable else a lie!"*

Good evening and welcome to yet another skill chapter- conclusion skill ! Let's go into the details.

Conclusions are final answer of your process, topic, arguments, thesis, research, study. Conclusion helps you to guide about the result of overall process. The success of all your hard work, preparation and efforts fall into the way you conclude the chapter. Let's see point wise the essentials of practical conclusions.

Conclusion Details:

- The wait of certification of mechanical test overs when you see result on the machine. When the test result found satisfactory as per given specification, the way the test carried out prove to be right and our conclusion become true.

- Most of the time in investigations and their analysis, different evidences are collected. Suppose in a failure of metallic part we observe intergranular crack, we are surprised to see these cracks, when we see its specification, material heat treatment at certain temperature range is suggested, when we observe its test certificate we see the test temperature is 50 degree lower and accordingly we come to conclusion that it is because of incorrect heat treatment of metallic part the intergranular cracks are developed.

- In a fit up of three to four components when we try to fit second part with fourth one, we find out that part is not getting fitted completely. We study the drawing for any error and found out part no one is not set as per given degree and it is shifted about three degree. This drift in orientation caused part number two to shift from its original position. This is the reason why both parts are not fitted properly. In the end, we replace & correct the orientation of part one as per the drawing and then check the assembly of part no two with part no four. The conclusion is error in set up caused the incorrect orientation.

- In a graphical analysis the data structure often help us to conclude about the status of data. A rising trend shows progress, a downward slope is mostly related to challenges and issues, a stable line means parameters are within limit and same monitoring is required to continue the status. The status of various chart often separate the data into its subtype which help us to take decision on specific area. In the end, conclusion derived from graphical analysis is like converting image into logical words to take corrective actions.

- The inability to derive conclusion is major lacuna Towards the path of leadership. In leadership, various uncertainties, difficulties, hurdles and risk occurs. As a leader you need to assess the situation clearly, derive future path with the help of options and then acting decisively. The perfect ability to conclude about the situation is fundamental step towards building strong leadership skills and strong team potential. Because strong leaders create great team and people learn by taking risk and using freedom.

- In typical leadership roles, data come in front of you in scattered form because you are representing a team and in a team there can be different views, inclinations and practices. Your job always remain to identify the truth behind every happening, its current and future impact on the business, definition of future as period of three years from now or ten years down the line, the need of initiation of change and its successive implementation, these steps guide you to conclude on the matter when the information is scattered and you need to decide on the basis of your judgment, experience, skill and confidence.

- When we feel surprised about how the leaders take decision in most of the toughest situations of their life, the timely acquired skill of small decisions, conclusion and learning act as their knowledge capital. Generally it is assumed that with more experience people become mature and they can sense the things before theyactually happen. With years people are used to face same or similar situations and sometime because of errors or because of success they come to know about the exact path of decision making and conclusion. In a typical difficult situation you will face lack of resourcefulness, lack of support, lack of clarity, lack of direction and still you have to find out your way with the help of the skill of conclusion making of prevailing situations.

Hope you like this chapter! Let's pause here!

SKILL 176 : FACE READING SKILL

PHOTO CREDIT : ALMOS BECHTOLD, UNSPLASH.COM

Dear Friends,

Good Morning and welcome to yet another skill chapter – face reading skill! Let's see into the details!

> *" Face reading is about knowing & guessing a person for his primary personality type to decide your response to a better interpersonal relationship !"*

Different personalities are present in this world. There are kind people, there are lovely people, there are determined people, and there are cool & calm people. How we identify & know the people before actually interacting with them? The skill is known as face reading skill!

Psychologically, whatever is going out in a mind is seen on persons face and his eyes. We say eye's never lie and with general know how about this technique we can arrive at primary conclusion about a person's way of general public behavior and success of your relation.

Let's see point wise what is face reading?

Face reading skill :

- It is not our intention to observe the face in first interaction but some indications display basic personality type. A kind & honest person always has calm presentation of their overall interaction with people. These people will always put peoples benefit first. They are very very clear and like to be treated equally by others. They smile often, listen well and appreciate your views with candid interaction. During conversation they will smile often and make your conversation lively. Post your first interaction, they will continuously remain in touch with you. They will inform you about latest event and make sure you are part of their team. They are inclusive people and like to associate with trust & loyalty. If something is not like out of your interaction, they will openly share their concern and seek improvement and they will offer their support.

- Arrogant people will have stubborn approach in their dealing. They will not smile nor show any first level interest while dealing with you. They will remain quiet and speak in disengaging manner. While discussion they will use inappropriate words and this will make you aware about their behavior. Their face is mostly neutral and you have to put great efforts to make them smile. Their voice tone is generally high and it may include some sharp words in their conversation.

Selfish and cheaters will act differently in different situations. To know such people, the first interaction is not enough; you have to carry out several interactions. When you deal with these people, they will put their benefit first and always discuss the things in which they have benefit. Actually selfishness is not wrong but anything excess is always unavoidable. Highly selfish people forget to think about the all the pros and cons of their decision and they tend to make one sided decisions. These people based on situation will show different expressions on their face, when they need something, they will come with a smiling face while we they don't have to do a certain thing they will show nervous face for some time. With their facial expressions, they will try to influence your decision in their favor and thus cheating with you emotionally.

- Analytical & investigative people will have a neutral face. They will not show any facial expressions like smile, laughter and most of the time their face look expressionless. If you review their conversation, you will observe there will be more questions and less answers. They will get information by various ways and make you keep talking till they receive what they need. If your seek their view on certain subject, they will speak shortly and to the point. If you insist them to speak more, they will not cooperate beyond a certain point.
- Co operative & supportive people has bright facial expressions. They smile often and always listen with engagement. They will nod in between conversation, will share jokes and make your conversation lively. In the conversation they will allow you to talk completely and they will listen quietly. In group discussion they will always support your view strongly and when require they will display open support in public places. They are clean and clear in their facial expressions and overall dealings. They are trustworthy and friendly. There is immense sense of security when you share something withthem. They are reliable and like to be treatedwith sincerity and positive approach in their relation.

Hope you like this chapter. Let's pause here!

SKILL 177 : BODY LANGUAGE SKILL

PHOTO CREDIT : SAM MOQADAM , UNSPLASH.COM

Dear Friends,

Good morning and welcome to yet another skill chapter – Body language skill! Let's see into the details!

> *"Body language convey approach. Body language represents current state of mind. Body language display interest!"*

We have seen facts about face reading in last chapter. This chapter add to yet another important skill in interpersonal interaction which is called as body language skill. Let's see point wise how this skill is to be developed.

Body Language Skill :

- A smiling face, clean and sober look, neatly combed hair, descent attire display a positive body language.
- Maintaining eye contact, nodding to point of acceptance and confronting with detailed study shows genuine interest in conversation.
- Any business deal happen with interpersonal communication. The common etiquettes which display courtesy, patient listening and asking questions & doubts about particular concept clarity display generous approach and sincerity.
- Hardworking and result oriented people will always walk fast and will do many things in same time frame. They talk less and focus more on getting things done.
- In a group meeting, people with positive body language will actively participate in meeting, they will provide suggestions and make meeting participative.
- When there are disagreements, person with positive body language will put the things on the discussion table and seek what is wrong and how it can be corrected.

- In challenging situation, a daring approach and thoughtful initiative resolve difficulties and make our ways clear. The benefit of daring is we remover all thought of fear and failure and so we have to focus only on resolving problem. The benefit of thoughtful approach is our actions are clearer and they lead to logical results.
- The typical dialogue delivery has affirmative voice, this voice provide you sense of security. This voice is friendly and never dominate your thought process. The conversation with affirmative voice goes long in interpersonal relationship development and this body language become the symbol of co-cooperativeness.
- What happens when people ignore you, don't mix up with you, and resist your thoughts? These questions are also important to know about how we should not display some negative body language indicator. If you are not maintaining eye contact it suggest you are not sure on what you are talking. Dominating other persons view constantly will make him angry and the discussion could become a waste of time. When people are resisting your thought by showing disagreement, you have to listen patiently andmake sure you convey your point with confidence and determination. If you also start argument, the discussions turn into quarrels which make environment unfriendly and non-participative.

- In a developed work culture, people have given responsibilities and they own their work. There are always scope for improvements and even though mistakes happens, people give second chance for improvement. These mistakes are considered as new learning and this is shared with group unanimously to communicate common learning. Openness of communication and consultation make people feel supported and such team always display a vibrant body language.
- Place a laughing character in serious group and see how he enlightens the scene. Place a quite person in entertaining group and he how he learns to mix up and gel with friends. Place a shy person in adventures group and see how he tackle various challenges coming his way. The point to convey is that our personality development is continuous process and we keep developing according to sphere of influence. Many body language indicators are knowingly or unknowingly inspired from people around you. Regional customs are best example of same. We see some countries greet with bow while some greet with handshake. We greet with Namaste! These indicators are best examples to display respect,
- Love and cultural harmony. Body language should naturally show these customs. Benefit positive body language are abundance and we have to learn them every day.

Hope you like this chapter! Let's pause here!

SKILL 178 : HANDSHAKE SKILL

PHOTO CREDIT : CHRIS LIVERANI , UNSPLASH.COM

Dear Friends,

Good Morning & welcome to yet another skill chapter- Handshake skill! Let's go into the details!

> *" Handshake is the first feel of a person's confidence and warmth . A gentle and firm handshake starts therelation of trust ,support and co-operation!"*

In modern business culture handshake is become the first sign of confidence and co-operation. When its deals, there is handshake. When there is agreement there is handshake. When you want to depart, you shake hands to meet again. When you start discussions, you start with handshake. When you party with your friends, your handshake is stylish and trendy. Let's see point wise the various situations and usage of handshake.

Situations where handshake is must:

- A new meeting is happening with your new client and you have invited your client to your venue. You come to know about their arrival and as per your custom, you go to receive them. When they come down out of their vehicle, you and your team greet them and welcome them with a firm, confident and medium paced handshake. You take care that you maintain positive eye contact with guest, rise smile on the face, warmth of personality and a welcoming approach to make them most comfortable in your environment in such a way that they will feel relaxed. Mind it, when we visit external places, everyone get little bit anxious about the environment. culture , custom . Everyone want to behave as per their natural liking however in a different environment people generally become concerned and hence might feel little bit shy . To remove this shyness, you have to approach them with a welcoming handshake and a candid dialogue. This makes your guest more open.

- In a second situation, you are a youngster and appearing for an interview with panel. You have been asked to enter in the interview room. You come inside the room with formal permission and greet the team with good morning. You go to individual and offer a firm and confident handshake. Panel like your initiative in connecting with new people and they also shake their hands with you. This is always a good start before starting an interview. This small step breaks the barriers of identity and makes you more promising and approachable. In the next phase, based on interview questions, you develop your professional identity and make your hiring decision simple. The smile on the face with positive eye contact and slightly lean composure reflect politeness in body language and same should be passed in subsequent handshake.

- When you are setting contract terms with your suppliers, your supplier offer you handshake. Now you are on receiver side. You should accept their co-operation with trust and honesty. This trust and honesty is reflected through a constantly engaged handshake. You speak one or two sentences which reflect your brotherly support with supplier. When your contractual terms are discussed and you are about to leave the meeting, you again strongly offer the handshake and promise to work together. Handshake is always associated with best compliments like thank you; this is great start, what a day today we meet here in this beautiful city. This

keeps interaction more friendlily.
- Friends, what will happen if we don't do handshake? This aspect is also very much important. If we don't do handshake before start of a new relation, we will not get the feel of person's real nature. The major physical interaction such as positive eye contact, gentle handshake , patient listening , voice tone all reflect your eagerness in the conversation , your genuine interest in the relation and your sensitivity is giving importance to traditional approach of personal touch and warmth .
- Rural places have lot of light cultural environment. Rural people instead of handshake offer their genuine respect and interest to new conversation with Namaste! The dialogue is very very friendly and new introduction always happens with complete team .These people are very charming and there are instances that conversations are often friendly and new guest are welcomed with lots of enthusiasm, happiness and hospitality. People believe in friendship and their maturity level is great in making new people comfortable in the environment. In informal introduction handshakes can be trendy and stylish based on youthfulness!

Hope you like this chapter! Let's pause here!

SKILL 179 : DEALING WITH UNCERTAINITY SKILL

PHOTO CREDIT : HANS PETER GAUSTER, UNSPLASH.COM

Dear Friends,

Good noon and welcome to yet another skill chapter- dealing with uncertainty skill. Let's go into the details!

> *"Uncertainties create hurry and mismanagement. As an experienced manager and skilled leader you have to think a little beyond to think about managing uncertainties!"*

Friends, your sales increased 30% and you are required to increase your production capacity by 50% with recent business forecast! How you will serve in this situation?

After consistently fulfilling targets, your business is experiencing 20% fall in demand! How will you respond to ensure your achieve your annual business plan?

You are manufacturing a new product and during testing it pass all tests and now you are planning to launch it in the market and suddenly a competitor's new product come into the market. Will your sales affect?

You are collaborating in a technology tie up. Your plant will be utilized for its manufacturing and assembly while technology partner will supply the technology. You share a very good understanding and after several years of association you have fostered this bond with new product and new techniques. Now new rules of international co-operation are formed in which your stake may be reduced. Will you continue the bonding?

People in your organization are working with you for several years and with inauguration of new facility in your industrial area they are finding new opportunities to join. There are possible chances of huge attrition and you need to carry out large scale recruitment. Will you allow the workforce to leave or you will make them happy by raising their salaries?

Friend's uncertainties are as certain as the day and

night, we can't escape from it without facing them. There is definite way of dealing with uncertainties.

Let's see point wise how uncertainties are dealt.

- First analyze the impact of the uncertainty. Then plan for impact response.
- Situations are temporary, find out quick solution to buy some time, once things settled, plan for its systematic resolution.
- Survival in the toughest time is the result of patience, perseverance, hard work, knowledge and out of the box thinking. Apply these skillsets to ensure you manage uncertainty in front of you. You will come out of it.
- There will be supporting forces and restrictive forces, you have to use them to deal with situation. It rarely happens when you don't have any support. In a rarest situation in which you are not capable of getting help, just hang on and put your best efforts there.
- A thoughtful analysis and regular review of situations give you an idea about the changes. Every market gives your prior indication, every news is result of number of coincidences, every situation has a background, when you understand this linking, you have to observe the type of uncertainty and then decide its plan of action.
- There is fix amount of time in which uncertainties exist, after this time things become clear and we can find the solution path. But the energy required to

stay on the ground for that particular stage is called as courage and stamina. This is unique potential.

- The attitude to combat with uncertainty is the result of constant efforts to resolve problems in small steps slowly and steadily . In a volatile environment the long term approach has to be supported by instant plans with various options. You have to think in three directions- if things happen as per plan what will be my response , if thing doesn't happen as per my plan what will be the response and if things happen in completely unknown way , how I will ensure minimum loss or damage to me or my work or my image . Simple! Once you start thinking critically, we find way to deal with it!

- It is best practice to save in your high time and use a part of it in challenging times . The regular habit of partial saving , right expenses and limited fun provides you the financial and resource security to maintain a healthy atmosphere in any uncertainties. Money is supreme resource in practical material world and we have to earn it with all good way and utilize it in best possible way . When you have time, people and money , you can overcome any uncertainty. We have to remember every new invention is victory over uncertainties and hence with scientists mind and scientific approach we have to carry out our actions.

Hope you like this chapter. Let's pause here !

SKILL 180 : PLEASANT INTERACTION SKILL

PHOTO CREDIT : RAM KATNENI , UNSPLASH.COM

Dear Friends ,

Good afternoon and welcome to yet another new skill chapter- Pleasant interaction skill ! Let's go into the details !

> "*Pleasant interactions are the result of valid points, generous listening and effective timing relevant to reality ! Its important skill to create influence and identity!*"

Technical skills in the field are built up with constant study , experiments and discussion advancement with peer group . Development of management and leadership skill happen with actually working with people . On a typical fine day , a manager has to listen to number of people and he has to report to their seniors along with factual analysis , data and his conclusions to make his senior decide the matter and taka a final call in least possible time and again focus on business urgencies.

In a typical month end pressure a leader had to direct his team in least amount of time and every time instructions not work . Modern leadership has to sensitively discuss the issues with their teams and suggest the right options immediately. With availability of technology and internet the knowledge is become easily accessible and it only requires the sense of timing to take right decision. If you are able to read the current situation and take a right decision , you have passed the daily performance test.

When you are dealing with your customer , your discussions revolves around delivery schedule , payment schedule , technical breakthroughs, yours long term association and the trust level created in this period. With every dialogue you allow time to customer to gel with your commitment to serve for him. This build up robust belief in your potential and in your ability to arrive at result in best possible ethical way . Such true, honest interactions are always meant to carry a great level of understanding and support in times of crisis.

Interaction with your team member during sharing his new of promotion is most pleasant one . You share with him the performance highlights and why management decided to offer you new position. This interaction also accounts for performance expectations in new role and with this you foster a strong bond of trust and equal opportunity . You have to listen his response also. Maybe he is happy with promotion if it is happened in time. If there is any delay , he will not speak directly but indirectly he will share his concern . In such situations , you have to talk sensitively and assure full support in coming times . Pleasant interactions always end with hope and aspirations.

Many times when you invest time in developing good relations with people working with you , you come to know fine details about their personality . The ability to talk and freely , comfortably and genuinely is the fundamental aspect of managing teams. In every interaction you come to know about the issue , its background, the role of concern parties and the miss out in role because of which issue is created . All you have to do is memories the process , find out the reason behind opposite stand and work out a time bound solution by walking that extra mile. This extra is always accountable . This effort is main deciding factor when you compare normal interactions and pleasant interactions. A leader always ensures he spreads positivity ,hope and collective wisdom .

On contrary, what will happen if interactions are not pleasant. A negative thinking always tells us the reason of acceptance of positive thinking . If the interactions are not pleasant, people will not feel comfortable in dealing with you . They will become reserve . They will not share complete details and hence you will never have faithful conversation . People will pass the buck on each other and this will consume lots of time of system.

There will be harsh arguments and debates and in all this situation the brand image will be at stake . The idea and creativity will be reduced and people will work without sincere commitment . There will be errors and errors that will increase rework and spend hell lot of time in achieving timely deliveries. When people are conversing without trust the information can be used for wrong purpose and many times it can be misused . You will be surprised to see how this negative energy is part of your system and how difficult it is to come out of that situation .

To avoid all these consequences , we have to practice positive approach and pleasant interactions. Talk with respect , knowledge and love and see how the other person will respond to you. People like to be loved , to be cared , to be guided , to be supported and to be understood. As a manager or leader , its half part of your profile to understand people and situations to devise right solution . Once you set this norms and standards ,people enjoy working with you always!

Hope you like this chapter! Let's pause here!

SKILL 181 : SUPPORT SKILL

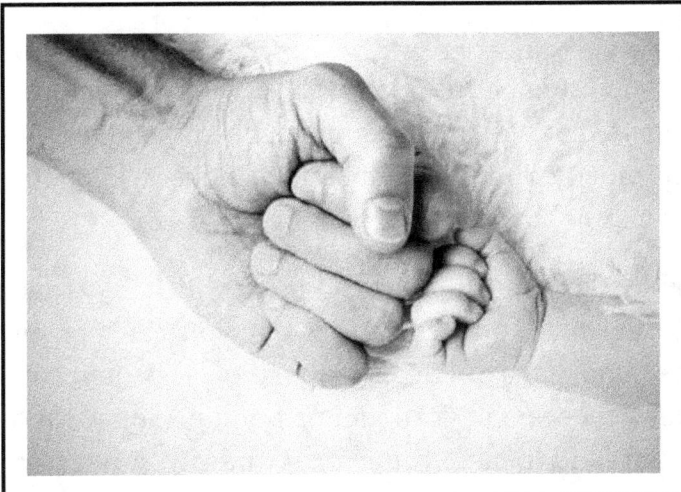

PHOTO CREDIT : HEIKE MINTEL , UNSPLASH.COM

Dear Friends,
Good morning and welcome to yet another skill chapter- Support Skill! Let's go into the details!

> *" Support plays important role in getting things done quickly . There are limitations on individual contribution but with several hands of support engaged in noble work, the work itself become an exemplary model of progress!"*

How many things one can do individually?

You can write on your own but somebody need to teach you writing at first!

You can drive a vehicle but somebody has to train & certify you to claim you are a better driver!

You may start a company to develop & deliver the products that will fulfill people need and make you earn some money, but you alone can't make it happen, you need people to work with you, work for you!

You have to deposit money in bank which is earned out of hard work and dedication, but you can't protect it alone, you have to take support of a strong banking system where you can deposit your money in your account and hence you can withdraw it as per the requirement.

Friends, support is critical. Support is must. Support is required. Support is the act of participating in co- working to achieve common result. If you are working together and if you don't achieve your results, it means you put less efforts and your support system is also not very very effective.

If you review any organization structure, you will observe there is fix systematic linking of various authorities. The main leader is supported by department heads. Department heads are supported by their internal team members. The cross functional activities are supported by defined role and responsibilities. Who will support whom in which situation is clearly defined and this is implemented in day to day situations.

When people work together, there are chances of having some differences, disagreements and concerns. To receive support from every team member there are some prerequisite to approach people. Approach with positive & friendly communication, listen first –then put your views, try to arrive at logical conclusion, take the people into confidence and seek their support, out of ten people, try to receive genuine support of at least 6-7 people as five fingers are the hands are not equal but when we have to life something we have to come together! This life principle has to cherish in receiving and providing support. When there is work, we have to come together as an unit, when work is over; we have to live in friendly manner respecting individual freedom and priorities.

It is so common that people ask for support. The issue is if everyone is preoccupied with their work they may not able to support or if the interpersonal relation in between people is not healthy they may not support each other. When we dig deep we observe the level of comfort enhances support. Means to get and receive support from people, your personal dealing with them has to be friendly, helpful and loyal. You should share things with your team member and make them feel they are part of an integral unit. When it is about working ina dedicated team, you have to put benefit of team first and then your personal goal. This keep you supported in all situations!

To understand the importance of support, let's see what will happen if you not receive support at right time!

A person is met with an unfortunate event and he is not admitted to hospital, there may be a life risk!

You are working on a project and one of your departments not delivered their result because they not received input in time from other department, the internal miscommunication result in failure of team's deadline and in such situation nobody is receiving any benefit. It is the matter of inefficiency and non-co-cooperativeness. Instead it could have happened that whatever work is there same could be discussed jointly, same could be planned in steps and same could be monitored for its joint completion. This could have displayed as perfect example of co-working and providing support to each other.

People generally refuse to support because they believe they do not receive their due credit and their credit is stealing by other people. This is quite logical and in the start of the process, we have to discuss the mutual benefits of supporting each other. We have seen number of examples of purchaser and supplier interpersonal cooperation. On an agreed purchase terms, supplier supply parts which make purchasers activity timely and correctly. This helps to achieve fast growth! Hope you like this chapter! Let's pause here!

SKILL 182 : EXTRA VALUE ADDITION SKILL

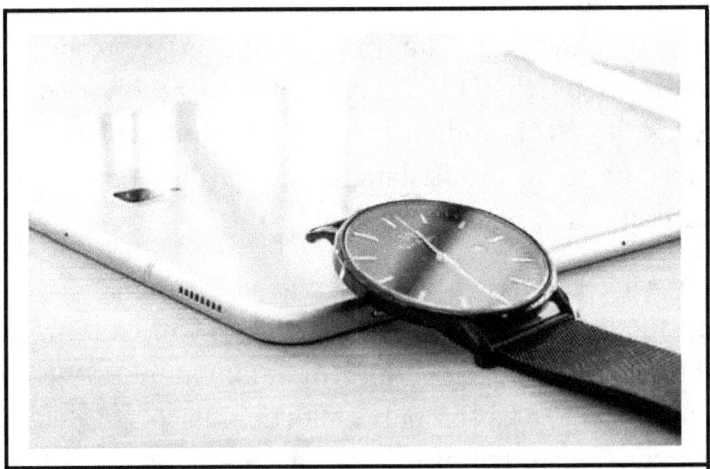

PHOTO CREDIT : OBI ONYEADOR , UNSPLASH.COM

Dear Friends,

Good Morning and welcome to yet another skill chapter- Extra value addition skill! Let's go into the details!

> " *Value addition enhances the original scenario ! It isthe important contribution that changes the properties to much desired level!*"

What do we mean by value addition?

Friends we work together to achieve desired targets. Everyone put their whole hearted efforts. In a good caring culture people support each other, contribute jointly and resolve problems with logical discussions and right actions. The value addition is nothing but collective participation as a team to resolve complex issues. It is this individual contribution which help to win your team in challenging situations. Let's see few examples of value addition!

In a cricket match, everyone plays nicely in a run chase and finally the situation come where you have to score 18 runs in six balls. The inform batsman takes the strike for four balls and the pair collectively score 19 runs. So this timely contribution acts as major value addition. Here all previous score and innings has no use If you are not able to score difficult target under pressure of run chase , so the last batting pair is always a major contributor.

In second example, a super performer is master of all trades and he can represent any work location as easily as the regular person can. He has acquired this skill with practicing and getting trained at various positions and in different situation. When there is absentee or urgency, this performer leaves his work and attends the urgency, ensure the urgency is met and again join his work. Because of his selfless working habit, he has developed two people who take care of his work in partial form to make sure he also achieve his targets.

This whole group adds value to their function. Can we account value addition?

Yes, we can certainly account for value addition. The difference in result , the saving of cost , the enhancement of aesthetics, the ease of working on challenging assignments with certain people , the experience and its correct utilization as per situation is example of visible value addition.

There are few peoples in the team whose mere presence also acts as value addition. These people inspire the team, motivate them to cross their limits of performance and cheer up in milestones and achievements. These people are nothing but important contributors to value addition.

How a project manager adds value?

He monitors every situation right from kick off meeting to handing over of the project to its customer. In meantime he constantly supervise, guide, assess, delegate , strategize ,allocate task and responsibilities with every stake holders right form designer , purchaser, supervisor , quality engineer, customer contact , site supervisor, statutory authorities . His every word is important as far as the project progress is concerned.

How a worker adds value? He has limited role and limited responsibility yet his work is main indicator of your firm's market identity and visibility. A beautifully crafted product the first impression in the minds of customer and the whole credit of converting paper drawing into exact replica of physical product goes to every worker. If you have seen the sincerity in shaping every curve shown on the drawing you will observe that handling the machine is not so easy. The hand eye coordination required while maintaining desired dimensions is very very difficult and it requires whole hearted attention. This craftsmanship is certainly the work of good value addition to team.

How a security guard adds value?

Throughout the day , he observe your visitor , record in and outs, talks politely and guide your guest to land at your work location . In a big organization where there are thousand employees and several workplaces, entry to visitors is always limited to their desired destination. These people sincerely take your guest to person with whom they wish to meet. When there is material entry and material exit, they ensure accurate recording of vehicle number and paper invoices. This check is very much important and it act as first check point in any issues related to material loss or theft. Security person has developed keen eye to face reading and they immediately respond to inappropriate demands and entries. Have you ever seen security person talks like a receptionist? Never, they will always ask questions to their visitor, verify the identity and then they will provide the access. This is great value addition to your systems security. Hope you like this chapter! Let's pause here!

SKILL 183 : MIS CREATION SKILL

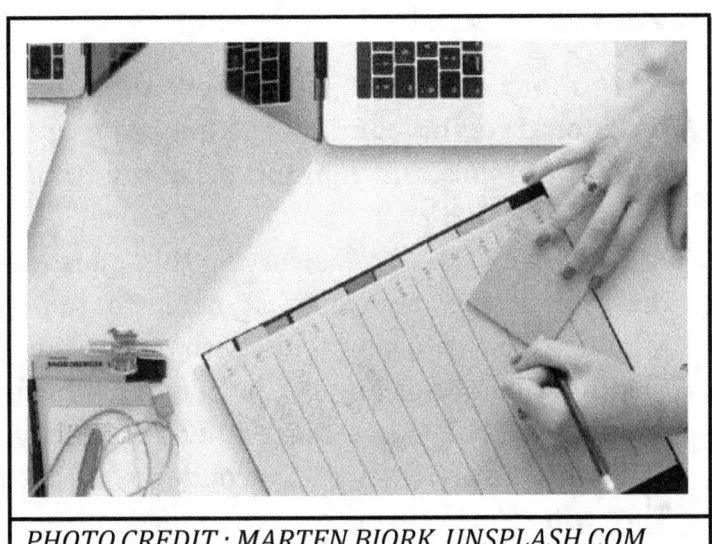

PHOTO CREDIT : MARTEN BJORK, UNSPLASH.COM

Dear Friends,

Good Morning and welcome to yet another skill chapter- MIS creation skill! Let's go into the details!

> " *MIS helps management to get information about monthly performance . Its parallel way of measuring your system efficiency along with your day to day review !*"

MIS is one form of information system in which monthly performance is shared with your seniors and the team. Let's see point wise how MIS is generated and maintained!

<u>MIS Generation Basics:</u>

1. **How many times it happened that a cross functional team complains that you are not doing your job and making so many errors in whatever you do ?**

    Friends, daily MIS is answer for this question. At the end of the day, make it habit to same ten minutes to back up your work with MIS. In this MIS, mention the jobs or units or projects on which you worked today. Prepare the schedule of activities and mark the activities which you done for that day. This will keep you up to date and make sure to answer your critics. Also make sure, you record errors happened during working to quantify the claim. Data is important asset and hence it is to be used with caution and care!

2. **How to produce MIS?**

    MIS is produced with various trackers. In these trackers you take a process, divide it in important milestones and on completion of milestones you mark it as done. Here because of online constant tracking you remain focused and if your tracking method covers every aspect that influence the completion of project then it is very very easy to initiate a trigger by which you can monitor and control the activities or you can communicate to your stakeholders.

3. **Are graphs necessary in MIS?**

   Yes graphs are required and must to present your MIS in best visual form. Graphs make you plot your data according to its different variables. You can easily find out relationship between these variables with visual review. The ups and down in the performance are easily seen in the data and Graphical MIS also act as symbol of certainty. Because graph is mathematical picture which has well defined X axis and well defined Y axis , so the decisions made out of graphical data follows mathematical relationship in the form on equation of line along with its slope and co-coordinators and based on the trend certain level of extrapolation can be done . It means, if the graph is showing continuous upward trend for sales, you can extrapolate the same for period of one quarter based on business dynamics and your own demand data booked for next quarter. In next stage you focus on increasing your span and by which you can ascertain region wise order booking and sales prospectus.

4. **What will happen if I create wrong MIS?**

   In a collaborative network , MIS is produced by several functions independently and it is combined at the dais of your central MIS manager which is generally The CEO of the organization. Suppose you are carrying out a debit –credit MIS . If you record the figure of monthly expenditure as 10 Lakhs on various heads and if finance person records the same figure as 10 Lakhs and 100 Rs , then at the Dias of MIS manager , this difference of 100 Rs will be cross checked and necessary input is given to party who has missed the calculation . The month wise screening of business performance by this way help a CEO to align all of their functions in same line and if there are any fumble or miss-outs same can be balanced at common Dias at the end of the month. The basic purpose of creating MIS is data based decision making which will be accurate, reliable and quick.

5. **Is there easy way to create MIS ! We encounter consistency issue !**

    This is common problem with MIS generation . You have to develop the habit of sparing ten to fifteen minutes daily , or one hour weekly or two hours per fortnight or one four hour session per month to record your performance . Generally habit of daily recording is best and it ensures daily back up of your work . If you miss the data recording today , you have to ensure it is done next day or next to next day . The more gap you will create in recording , there will be major miss out in accuracy of the data . Hence it is necessary to create MIS regularly as it is the best indicator of your consistency and discipline which is required to function effectively. Friends, hope you like this chapter!

    Let's pause here!

SKILL 184 : RATING CREATION SKILL

PHOTO CREDIT : TENGYART, UNSPLASH.COM

Dear Friends ,

Good Morning and welcome to yet another skill chapter -Rating Creation Skill ! Let's go into the details!

> " *Rating help you know democratic positioning of product or service . The feedback given by people or consumers or customers are grossly genuine and they also influence your future sales prospectus in modern economy !*"

Friends, in modern digital age , people participation in online activities is increased to great extent . In the age of websites , applications and commercial advertisements , feedback about product or service become essential know-how before starting purchase activities.

In traditional purchase activities , we have guided about how to purchase items and necessary things in day to day life . There is always instruction to screen the market , visit four to five places to enquire for rates and the product quality . Discuss the deals with vendors and carry out possible negotiation . Package the product correctly so it's handling will be fine . And then make the purchase . The publicity happened was based on person to person communication . Suppose your friend want to buy a house in your area, he always used to ask about the locality , facilities , nearness to important landmark and overall community life . The type of builders and their successful projects , the infrastructure quality and opportunities for personal development for children's . Based on their feedback , you use to visit the actual developer and start cross checking the facts and feedback . The moment it matches to what your friend has suggested , you trust the rest of the things and make a buying decision . Now when you declare this decision with your friend circle , the other friends or their friends who are interested in new property enquire with you or visit you personally to know more about the project . You do same thing which is done by your friend . They do same thing which is done by you while making a purchase decision . So now developer is facing lots of enquiry about the project and hence the satisfied customers are providing business opportunities to expand their sales . This was about creating favorable rating and managing the business.

In current times , ratings are created with fact based surveys . You purchase a product or avail a service and at the end of the purchase you are asked to provide feedback in systematic options which display your inclination, interest and liking for the product or service . Generally this liking is based on increased level of satisfaction or dissatisfaction . The way you design the survey sheet , the way you get the response from people . It is always a best choice to keep a blank place to record any other reasons while providing a standard feedback template .

In a typical online commercial website , products are listed along with their product catalogue and latest photographs. People buy these products and provide feedback about the product when they receive physically . This feedback is reflected in product catalogue and generally this rating act as primary indicator of products popularity . It is common understanding that when majority likes a thing , it means the thing is made for the people and people feel it is relatable to their needs .

How to improve the ratings ? The basic answer to this question is two way . One way you have to ensure you prepare and produce excellent quality products and service. It should be good value addition to peoples need . Secondly you should master the skill of online positioning of your product . People should be aware about the latest happening on common social media with which they can review your product on the go . You have to cross check negative feedback in your system and present your finding . This clarity act two ways , one way it shows you are completely clear and transparent in your approach and secondly you answer people who unnecessarily provide wrong feedback.

The initial five years period is crucial for any new firm . This period is about establishing your brand . In this phase you will be have less customers and you need to provide more focus on your product development . The cope the competition , you decide your investment plan and carry out activities which focus on achieving a regular customer base . The discussion with customers, the details with which you take their care and the way your product simplify the things matter the most to customers . In this phase you must work on getting what customer need and the commercial aspect of delivering the same . You have to think constantly on options by which a safe and reliable product is created.

Ratings subject to change and this depends on your performance. When you focus on your performance , you don't need to bother about rating . You will remain at the top till the time you are one step ahead of your competitor.

Hope you like this chapter ! Let's pause here!

SKILL 185 : GENERAL KNOWLEDGE SKILL

PHOTO CREDIT: CHRIS LAWTON, UNSPLASH.COM

Dear Friends,

Good Morning and welcome to yet another skill chapter- General Knowledge skill! Let's go into the details!

> " *General knowledge is the know how about what's happening around us at various level like local, district, state , national & international . This aspect broaden our thinking and make us aware about the environment in which we live !*"

General knowledge is an important aspect of our life! Yes, since we become aware about the society in which we live, it become vital to know about the locality and people around us. As a student knowing the local administration, structure of our city or town or village, prominent people in our area and their contribution to society is very much important to know as it guides us to perform with right approach and right direction. Let's see point wise how this knowledge is acquired step by step.

Building General Knowledge:

- Reading & observations are two important aspects with which general knowledge skill is acquired. You have to read a lot and observe the environment around us about how it behaves.
- In a day to day life many things keeps happening in social sphere. When we are busy in our personal work or professional duty, in large sphere of society, bunch of incidences happen every moment. Newspapers, Television media and now internet is acting as main information provider for general knowledge.

When it is society then there are different sections or part of society. Society has education sector, politics sector, finance sector, geographical sector, historical sector, arts and cultural sector, sports and hobby's sector. Once you are clear about this specific pattern of the society then it is very very easy to study and learn general knowledge.

- Take one sector and read a lot about event. Where the event is happened, who were the participants, what was the highlights of the event, what is the importance of this event to society, when you will start asking questions to event information, you will be able to remember those link.
- Not everyone can have interest in all field , here you have to keep in mind that your favorite subject will never bore you and hence it is very important to know about your favorite subject and become an expert in that field.
- General knowledge is big knowledge bank and to become successful you have to deposit fact penny every day so that at the end of the month or year you can have a better deposit and which you can use for your optimum purpose.
- General knowledge is not only about events and special achievement by the people it is also about changes happening around us from time to time. If some drastic change is about to happen, we get its information from respective instant media sources. There is network ofgetting information from various authorities or authorities inform officially for publicawareness about changes supposed to happen and which will alter the way people lead their normal life. Hence having such knowledge is not only important but necessary.
- The knowledge about environmental changes and its impact is important one. If there is heavy raining and if we are planning our three day business trip in which we have to visit vendors workshop, lot of time

will be wasted to wait for rain free time and hence there will be element of inconsistency. We have to keep all updates about the route from which we are going to carry our journey. Secondly, if something happens suddenly, we have to plan for alternative way out. This knowledge also come from experiencing similar situations from past.

- Sometimes it is important to know about who is the winner, what was the prize money, who was the participant, which country sponsored the event, but more than that what importance sport play in our life and do we practice the sport regularly is an important point to know.
- General knowledge competitions now days provide thrill and excitement along with knowledge sharing. We have to participate in such event and test out knowledge. For every competition, we need preparation and understanding of terms and conditions of competition. When we know the rules of the game then only we can play the game safely. This wisdom is come from participating in such competitions from early age.

Friends, hope you like this chapter! Let's pause here!

SKILL 186 : EXIBITION BOOTH SETTING SKILL

PHOTO CREDIT : DEVAIAH MALLANGADA , UNSPLASH.COM

Dear Friends,

> *"Exhibitions are meant for branding and participation! It's best networking method and away to present your products to huge audience attending the exhibition!"*

Good Morning and welcome to yet another skill chapter- Exhibition booth setting skill! Let's go into the details!

Friends', marketing is important part of selling your product. Various social organizations calls for social exhibition events in which you get ample opportunity to showcase your products and make people physically attend the stalls and hence try some sales happening over there .For regular sales you can always present them your address and contact details . Nowadays because of digitalization of market such exhibitions happen through online mode in which customer can participate for limited sales period and buy the things he likes with either discount or with some offers!

Let's see point wise, how the product or service is displayed in exhibition booth.

Exhibition booth setting skill:

- Know about the event and plan early. Surf the event website or official platform where you can understand the rules of participation.
- Some exhibitions which presented in a stadium or open place charges some entry fee and nominal rent for running your booth. This fee is according to location of booth. Select the location as per category arranged by organizer. It means if it is electronic accessories row, you cannot set your booth of mechanical component near them. You have to follow row allocated for electronics items. Basically exhibition organizer take great of how visitors will enter, what will make them buy, how the arrangement at exhibition can be made comfortable,

how people will engage with brands and how much space should be provided to each exhibitor to display their product or services.

- When you have booked the booth, arrange for its decoration with modern flex or painting banners, posters in a way that it attracts your potential customers. Here you have to take care that you display your brand correctly and visibly.
- Once the booth is decorated, next stage is setting your product right and make them accessible to people. There should be ample space for movement and you should able to move along with customer to present the product or provide information about the product in a group .The participative nature of exhibition make customer comfortable and after several enquiries he decides to buy.

When people visit your booth or stall, welcome them with normal welcome etiquettes. Graciously inform them about your offering, technical parameters and prices. Inform them about the current offers and ask whether they would like to buy this product now or when can they contacted. Provide them your contact details and if possible visiting card to arrange the appointment. If the person is interested and he would like to purchase on large scale they will also handover the business card and based on which you can follow up later. This is major advantage of participating in exhibition which makes you visible to industry people.

- Adhere to booth timing and ensure you open it early. The exhibitions are mostly organized on holidays and weekly off so as more people can participate in it. You have to start early and wait late if more customers are visiting. There is crowd flow rate depending on time. Generally in the evening post 4PM crowd gathers and it can remain up to 10-11 PM. In this peak period, you have to ensure that you present your product in clear and concise manner.
- Some exhibitions receive slow response in the start while better response as it progresses. Your job is to focus on complete schedule and explain the product to customer.
- Although parking and other facilities are provided by organizers, you have to take care of safely moving your product and make sure they don't get any damage when same is handled by huge chunk of people.
- The design of offers and discount should follow a holistic view. Since there will be large influx of customers you can offer them good discounts to boost sales. The popularity received in such exhibitions act as accelerator to your regular sale. If possible you can prepare a separate team to participate in such exhibitions happeningaround the nation and make your brand visible.

Friends, hope you like this chapter! Let's pause here!

SKILL 187 : INNOVATION SKILL

PHOTO CREDIT : WERNER DUPLESIS, UNSPLASH.COM

Dear Friends,

Good noon and welcome to yet another skill chapter- innovation skill! Let's go into the details!

> *"Everyone like new things which can be a new book, new song , new dress , new home ! Why? Its magic of innovation . People get bored with daily soap and hence they need some good change! This is where creativity meets with innovation!"*

Friends, innovation are basic concept of human development and leading a successful life. Innovation represents successful experimentation which makes our life easy. Every invention is an innovation to its previous status. Let's see with point wise details how innovation is represented for different career path.

The path of innovation:

- For a medical practitioner, innovation is the change in method of surgery. Such methods could reduce cost of surgery, increase accuracy and make quick discharge. The current use of robots in critical surgery is example of such technological innovations. These robots has made some outstanding surgeries which enabled doctors and surgeons to take quick decisions about critical surgeries with which patient can be treated with best possible treatment with fast recovery . Not only surgeries, but development of vaccines and drugs is also subjected to timely innovation. The critical illnesses for which there is no medicine till date are rapidly researched and breakthroughs are achieved to combat with the disease.
- For a technological professional innovation is combination of new observation and old practice. Converting mobile handset to pocket friendly computer was such an innovation. Here with the help of traditional light emitting diode display and use of operating system, smart phone system is developed and the result is in front of us. Now more and

more applications are created to convert daily living needs into mobile friendly processes and transactions. This way we are going close to make our daily life easy to live. The various satellite missions are implemented to ensure enhanced view of planet and ensure more security from external challenges. When a new mission is launched, there is team working on every little aspect which makes this mission successful. Here the selection of material, study of environment and empirical calculation involved in successful launch all form part of innovation. Because every time you have to apply same equations with variable conditions.

- For a creative person like an actor, a new role which has many shaded to its character always needs deep study and regular practice. When a big role such as a tremendous famous and popular character is offered to an actor, he has to read and study their biography through which he gets fair idea about their life. In next phase, they have to practice the behavioral traits and have to practice it so easily that people will love this kind of character presentation.

- For a new singer, a song based on ragas and having different tuning than his regular practice is always challenging. To achieve desired level of comfort in their performance, he has to practice for several hours on given raga, then he has to practice the lyrics and the tune, then they have to work on its rough trails with co-singers and chorus, the next step will be musical rehearsal and when all things are practiced correctly, the final recording of song in the studio. When the song is released after post production process, we get the gift of this innovation and new experiment is music field. When this experiment like's people the song become a massive hit and if the song is not liked by people, the music director has to try for other experiments. The thinking of a music director always follows a natural harmony of tunes to the vocal capability of the singer. When the singer is versatile and has very good & divine voice tune, getting song sung from him is a cakewalk and any difficult composition can be sing easily and clearly.

- Innovation for a sports person like a cricketer is number of playing shots or deliveries he fine tunes in his practice. We see various new deliveries are experimented which cannot be played easily and batsman get out. Also we see batsman innovate new ways of playing difficult deliveries and score even four and sixes. This is nothing but constant practice and improvement of skill with finding something unknown. This element of surprise always favor in actual match which keep you ahead of your competitor. When your creativity meets experiment correctly innovation emerges and makes you a solid winner!

Friends, hope you like this chapter! Let's pause here!

SKILL 188 : STATUS QUO QUESTIONING SKILL

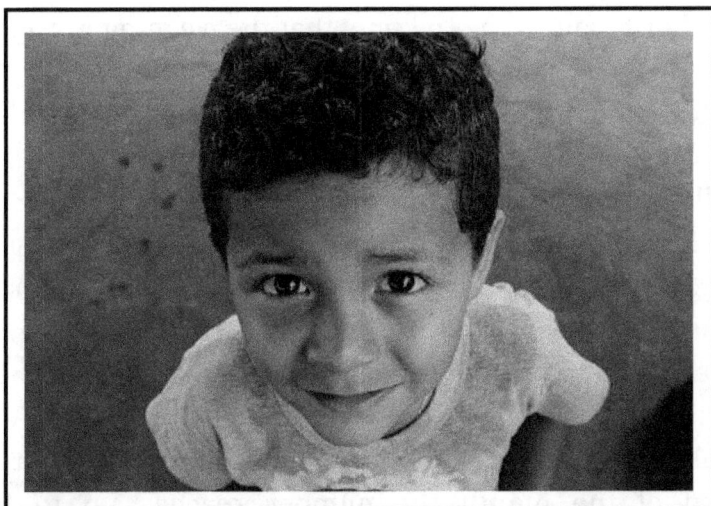

PHOTO CREDIT : DAVID RANGEL, UNSPLASH.COM

Dear Friends,

Good afternoon and welcome to yet another skill chapter – status quo questioning skill! Let's go into the details!

> " *Status quo questioning is about observing loopholes in current system and make sincere efforts to find a way out towards improvement and development!*"

Friends, we visit a garden on one of holiday and observe there is so much dirt, dust, polythene bags, eatables remains and scattered things. We feel surprised and question whether there any housekeeping is done or not? We check with garden authority and come to know that the cleaning is done in the morning and the second round will happen in the later evening! You feel quiet with the answer. This is because if there is cleaning done two times a day and sill there is so much garbage it means people are not following rules and same need to be conveyed in a civil and democratic way. What you do, you prepare a volunteer team and practice garden cleaning every weekend to create the picture of self-awareness. Initially you start with five to seven people but with passing time more and more people join you and at the end of the month the number reaches up to fifty members. What you do, without talking a single word to visitor, you simply clean the garden and support regular house keeper. Now because of one month's sequence people get aware and they start following basic rules and make less garbage as well as they ensure they don't carry unnecessary things with them. Friends, this is not a fiction. Such stories happen in reality. All it required is your ability to ask question to current status and make collaborative efforts to make relevant changes. Once you take intuitive slowly people support and participate with whole hearted contribution. Initially you may face problems, you may encounter resistance but it is your ability to discuss the matter in right tone and approach that make people work on such projects.

In office environment, suppose the workshop in which you are working is receiving one item form supplier and it is continuously coming with some problems because of which evertytime its fitment with your part is causing delays and issues. There is involvement of two to four different functions and issue lacks ownership and accountability. After noting this scenario and discussing with your seniors you call every concern people of common platform and put data of last six months issue with this part supply. In every instance you find out there are different issue owners. Sometime the issue is because of drawing, sometimes because of misfit and sometimes a critical check is missed in urgency or something like that. You present the number of hours your workshop worked to rectify these points and hence you have wasted a shifts time and your planned work is lagged because of this. When you sincerely portray the problem at your end, everyone promised to devise a common agreement on dispatch of part from vendor end. A dedicated vendor quality engineer will visit all vendors and prepare his inspection report with set quality norms which are followed in the workshop. He will provide detailed report and if he shows some suggestions, all vendors has to comply those before they dispatch the material. His inspection report is must when you supply the material and only after satisfactory acceptance of his report your material will be in warded. This agreement is done with respective vendors, their associated buyers, shop supervisors and vendor quality engineers. With common minutes of meeting you freeze the thing and make a process change to update the quality manual. With new process, you start receiving part with inspection report and exact matching to your parts. The vendor quality engineers has devised few exact template on which part is fitted , they carry out part to part trial and mock up assembly , they note serial numbers of mating part and same is mentioned in their inspection report . Now suppose there are multiple parts are received and numbers are mismatched, there is chance of wrong fit. To avoid this scene, a copy of inspection report is handed over to workshop for serial number reference and exact match is ensured. This way the proper alignment of system and inspection programme the assembly misfit problem which was long pending and time consuming was resolved with implementation of process change and documenting this change in the system.

Friends, if you are working in a system, you are always entitled to ask logical question which mention concern over current way of working, possible improvementand benefit to team because of new ways and approaches. If you fail to ask, you will limit your performance to certain boundaries and always follow what others ask for. To avoid such a stereotype personality, you have to build this skill of questing status quo!What will happen ? You will be ignored or wrong answers will be given , but its fine . You have to insist till you receive the right and correct answers . Friends, hope you like this chapter! Let's pause here!

SKILL 189 : NOW OR NEVER ATTITUDE SKILL

PHOTO CREDIT : ATTENTIE, UNSPLASH.COM

Dear Friends,

Good Morning & welcome to yet another skill chapter- Now or Never attitude skill! Let's go into the details!

> *"Promptness and diehard efforts are critical success factors when we deal with execution of work! Now or never attitude make you work with limitless strength and unidirectional focus to win in any situation!"*

Friends, we like cricket. In a typical championship, there is system of matches schedule and the qualification stages for next round. In a typical championship like World Series or world cup, global international teams participate in the event and they play with each other at least one time. What a beautiful concept this is!

In a typical world series, in the entry round teams play with each other . Some matches are easy while some matches are played hard. When the first round completes the status of all teams comes in front of us. If the next round involves entry of best eight teams then if there are 12-16 teams, the rest 4-8 teams are disqualified. Now just think how they must be feeling to disqualify in first round itself!

This is where the now or never attitude works! Team management and coach right from first match enter into the match with immense ability and desire to win the series and they play every match as if it is now or never situation. First they devise strategy with which they ensure minimum number of matches to be won to qualify for the entry to next round. Then they will study their competitors. Based on their past performance they have idea about the strength and weakness of all teams participated in the series. Hence they work their strong options where they can win easily. They focus on these matches and record their ultimate win. For difficult opponent, they study their game, observe how players score runs and how they can block these runs and take wicket. On batting side, they study their blowers and their current form and devise a strategy which is a perfect combination of attack & defense. With this preparation they face the match and play as if it is now or never situation. Now if the opponent recognizes this change in attitude, they will also put their best efforts which will make this match interesting and treat to watch. If they don't recognize, they fail short in their efforts and this makes other team win the match. In a high voltage match, till last ball the picture is not clear. Everyone fights in such a way that they hate to fail. They fight in every match as if they are playing in the final. The complete team is putting great efforts and they ensure they can win in every situation. This is the reason why such teams become successful and remain champions. Nobody can defeat them. So depending of winner's spirit and collective team efforts, team records their win. Now in the next qualifier round of quarter finals, eight teams fight together to enter into semi final. Here the competition is tougher and every team put their best to enter into semis. However when actual game is played many unexpected events happens which make team little bit disturbed. It is the role of team leader and key player to adjust to these changes swiftly and ensure they guide their junior members to play with heart, body, soul. The team which respond to changes in strategic and playful way becomes a winner!At the end of the quarter finals, when the four teams have moved ahead and four teams are disqualified, the next three matches are main attraction of the world championship. In the semifinal round, you are two steps away from championship. Every team has equal chance of win. With the same winning spirit you enter into the match. The now or never attitude make you think about winning the toss so that you can go with your plan A and if you lose the toss then you have to go with your plan B . If you win the toss and decided to bat first, you have to put great total on the board. If you win the toss and decide to bowl first, you have to stop opponent in less score. The second side requires either making faster run chase without losing wickets or getting opponent out quickly and record a big victory. The net run rate act as deciding factor in the championship and your match point and net run rate act as your entry tickets to big game – finals! So, semifinals are played with all vigor and energy and the best two team qualify for the final.

The big game, final is played with full energy. One thing is fixed before the match is played. Runner up prize is fix, whoever will lose will become a runner up. Nobody is there to compete for second spot. The fight is on for number one position. Here every ball is played with sincerity. The pressure level is higher and the performance in the final is remembered for long time, hence extreme efforts are put in the game. In the end the best team wins and they become the champion. This is nothing but the result of winner's attitude. They have used their potential in every match to record important wins! Friends, hope you like this chapter! Let's pause here!

SKILL 190 : PRACTICAL BELIEF SKILL

PHOTO CREDIT : VLAD, UNSPLASH.COM

Dear Friends,

Good Morning and welcome to yet another skill chapter- Practical Belief skill! Let's go into the details!

> " Practical's help us to implement theoretical concept ! Without practical's , theories cannot be established ! Practical belief comes with application of knowledge to proposed theory!"

Friends, theory and the practical are what a science student learns in his academic years. While theories are based on scientific principles, natural laws and systematic study of linkage between variables, practicals support these theories with physical representation of theoretical concept.

Let's see point wise the necessary skill to believein practicals:

- In books we read a lot about interpersonal skill and the way of communication with the people. But when we actually start speaking physically we come to know about how to create a funful, enjoying and meaningful conversation. In such conversation we talk with love and respect. The conversing person also responds with similar feeling. When you are talking with your friends, things look very very easy. There is humbleness, gentleness, care and humor .What if your conversation turns into a debate. Don't afraid, when you are talking with your fried, automatically he will sense your mood change and balance the conversation with his mature nature. He will listen to your arguments and they slowly respond in best possible way. But in no way he will argue with you the way you are debating. This is about balancing the conversation practically. Now these things cannot be written in the books as every person is unique and they have all right to express themselves as per the best social norms.

- Secondly, we read a lot about using a machine but when it comes to using the machine, we feel uneasy. This is because we have not handled machines regularly and we are under fear that if something happens wrong the machine will damage and hence we will have loss! The best practical method to use the machine is see its internal structure , get understanding of its main parts, understand the central logic of machine and then work with external command panel with which machine obeys your instruction . For your information when we make a machine on with the help of a prime mover just an electric or mechanical force, it starts working. In Off condition, the different parts of the machine are aligned with each other as per their static design, when we want to move machine the principles of dynamics acts on it. This is nothing but the result of applied mechanics. The people, who know the internal details, never handle machine with casual approach. They take good care of its operation and handle practically wheneverrequired.
- Theories state number of postulates but belief comes when we perform the practicals. In a welding journal, number of advances is displayed to make people aware about latest trends but when we actually work with these changes then only we come to know about its importance. For e.g. . organizations can devise new electrode and inform through such journals. When somebody

decides to buy it and use it on their job, they actually find its practical use. If they are able to work with ease, if they can save cost or if they reduce their overall time, we conclude that the material is better and useful. But if we found we don't get what is committed, we don't use that product till desired changes are done by its manufacturer. Sometimes development happens in intermittent stages. In such cases, as the stage come into existence, we have to adopt the same in our process. We keep receiving the updated versions and hence feel the path of improvement alongside. So, here we can say the actual claim is verified with practical usage of the product!

- In quality assurance and control function you have the major responsibility to certify the accuracy and design of the product. Here in some cases people try to influence you and may request you to go ahead with set understanding. But always remember, every job is new and it has to pass through all its performance test. Even though you know 1+1=2 , if it is written perform this action 100 times , you have to ensure whether you receive same answer 100 times , this is because every product is unique and every customer may be unique or not but his experience to practically use and accept your product will be unique. If he note defect, he will always raise his concern!

Hope you like this chapter! Let's pause here!

SKILL 191 : ORAL CALCULATIONS SKILL

PHOTO CREDIT : MICHAL , UNSPLASH.COM

Dear Friends,

Good morning and welcome to yet another skill chapter – oral calculation skill! Let's go into the details!

> " The charm of old day's calculations lies in viva or by heart calculations. In this method ,with command over basic mathematical concepts of addition , subtraction , division and multiplication ,we come to mathematical result!"

Friends, mathematics is one of the most entertaining and engaging subject. Mathematics is all about logic, calculation and decision making. The basic stage of strong mathematics skill is good hold on numerical system, tables and mathematical equations. When you possess good knowledge about addition , subtraction, multiplication and division , you come to know about practical applications of working together , leaving something for option , working with scale and reproducibility and they way to face your opposition .

Let's see point wise how oral calculations help toresolve practical problems.

Oral Calculation Skill Building:

- You are about to visit a distance place and you have given one hour to plan for this sudden trip . How will you manage the situation?

    If you are frequent traveller, you will resolve this situation in just minutes. In technological world, you are connected with your network members. People have association and contact with each other which help to plan their journey, tours and business meeting. The first thing you will note the distance of the place in your mind and if you are going with personal vehicle or vehicle arranged by the organization , you will calculate the tentative time required for the travel. Once you come to know this distance, you will book your room with your travel booking agent and reach the venue. You will attend your work and will return next day as per your plan.

In journey time, you may think about putting thing in front of the parties and find out your responses to their tentative questions. These calculations in your mind act as dress rehearsal and make your actual conversation easy because if you are thinking on correct way there is possibility that you will guess most of them correctly. Since you utilized journey time wisely, you will be prepared for actual conversation and this make your meeting successful. Since you have booked return ticket same time, there will be no problem in coming back. This way you manage the urgent situation in correct way.

- Suppose you are a seasoned professional welder and a workload is allotted to you and you have to complete the same without any defect in least possible time. There is no fixed timeline but all expectations are concentrated on working fast and accurate.

  You observe the work, measure the number of joint or length of joint and number of run required to carry out the welding. You check the WPS and choose the effective electrode or wire size to have fast and accurate welding for given dimensions. You check the status of the machine and look whether they are working fine. If there is any problem, you get it corrected. You are given an aid in the form of junior or assistant welder; you decide your plan with him and provide him some instruction about how he supposed to support him during actual work. When things are set, you start working. You adjust the machine parameters and within less than ten minutes, you start working rapidly. Since the quality of joint set up is correct, you don't have major problem in welding the joint. You calculate the time available before first break and divide your work in shift break hours and set your personal milestones of work completion. Means if you are welding ten joints in eight hour shift with 6 hours actual welding, 1 hour for preparation and one hour for break, you will ensure in five hours you will complete ten joints and in remaining one hour you will carry out finishing touches with the help of you assistant. This way you achieve you target in given time, you achieve both speed and accuracy. Along the line as you have communicated all fact to your assistant , he also learn lot of things simultaneously and when time come about handle the things on his own , he also perform in the same way.

So oral or by heart calculations are not about telling 15+17= 32 orally , vocally but to plan things correctly with mathematical approach involving time available for activity , resources available for activity and your own speed requirement to accelerate the activity . This helps you to grow faster and accurate!

Friends, hope you like this chapter!
Let's pause here!

SKILL 192 : PROOF GENERATION SKILL

PHOTO CREDIT : SINCERELY MEDIA, UNSPLASH.COM

Dear Friends,

Good Morning and welcome to yet another skill chapter – proof generation skill! Let's go into the details!

> " *Proofs act as real support of explaining what is happened during a crisis or difficulties. Many conflicts are resolved with the help of necessary proofs!*"

Friends, when we grow and start working, we encounter with proof creation process. Let's see how we accustomed with proof creation with these point wise details.

Proof Generation Skill:

- **Identity Proofs:** Whenever we visit for interview or professional exhibition or seminars, the access to this location is based on the individual identity. Our I-Card act as basic proof of our personality. It reflects our identity details in the form of legal name, date of birth, our address and contact no. This proof act as traceability major in case of any identity related concerns.
- **Drawing Proof:** When we produce something, we always have some written guidelines in the form of a procedure or drawing. The engineering part drawing is basic document which act as valid proof with which part is made. Every part has it drawing number and applicable revision with respect to changes that happen from time to time. When there are conflicts about manufacturing process or any defect in the products, the part drawing is referred for further analysis. There is famous notion with respect to drawing and its usage. You can either make job as per your drawing or your drawing has to be same as per your job, any change in job or drawing has to be implemented in job or drawing. Suppose some unauthorized changes are done in the job by some people knowingly or unknowingly, it

is the approved drawing with which these changes can be highlighted, investigated and corrected. Suppose a part drawing has error with respect to its main drawings, the part will be manufactured accurately, however when you will go for its assembly, you will find misfit. To analyze this error, you check the main drawing and conclude that the error is happened because of error in part drawing. You correct both part drawing and job according to main drawing and resolve the issue with proof of main drawing.

- **Test Certificate Proof :** The test certificate is main document which tell you complete details about the material of construction , governing code of construction , testing carried out with product and test results, the material grade and its composition, apart from manufacturing the special treatment carried out for protection of material properties , the nomenclature and physical identification along with batch and serial number , the stamp of authority approving the part for its completeness and accuracy and seal of the manufacturing firm . Finally the disclaimer mentioning the scope of supply from your side and risk associated with transit and insurance. This certificate is used to correlate received material. In case of any miss out or mis placement, with the help of serial number we can check all process variables. This proof is generated online and when actual production is carried out. All test results are supposed to enter after immediate test and hence they are believed to be true and reliable.

Material clearances at the supplier & receiver end happen with the help of this documentary proof. If there is error in TC or error in physical punching, same need to be highlighted and corrected.

- **Commercial Invoice Proof:** When a transaction happens, along with material test certificate you receive tax invoice from supplier. This invoice mention the details of part identification, quantity, weight, its unit price, overall price, applicable taxes and their value, total amount in word and numbers along with yours firms official logo and trademark. The address of shipping and purchaser details, official seal of the supplier firm and any supporting documents which mentions the terms and conditions of supply. With this document, we can easily trace out the parts produced in a particular month, their payment status and there remark when the parts are received. If there are any payment related issues, we can trace the status with finance after providing the invoice details and payment history.

Friends, proof generation is important to keep you safe & secure while working and living.

Hope you like this chapter! Let's pause here!

SKILL 193 : LEGAL IMPACT SKILL

PHOTO CREDIT : MIKHAIL PAVSTYUK, UNSPLASH.COM

Dear Friends,

Good afternoon and welcome to yet another skill chapter – legal impact skill! Let's go into the details!

> *"Understanding of law of the land is main thing in carrying out business . When we adhere the business rules and associated laws, we ensure legal protection and authentic brand image!"*

Friends, carrying out business in legal environment require understanding of various rules, regulations and laws which are made in the interest of society as whole to ensure fair use and safety of people along with protection of business interest. The laws are formed with basic purpose of awarding justice to diseased and avoiding unlawful behavior of individual or firm while violating terms & clauses of the law. Let's see various legal impacts pertaining to business environments.

Legal Impacts and their awareness:

- Your purchase order is your official legal document and in the event of conflicts this act as proof for ensuring terms & conditions of supply. Both parties have to agree these terms before releasing & approving work order. In case there are any changes or amendments, we have to approve it with mutual agreement. Any unsolicited change in the terms of supply is simply regarded as breach of trust and when the matter reaches to Hon. Court you have to present the proofs and details regarding the transaction to prove your point. At the end of the legal proceeding what you get is compensation to your claim and enhanced reputation of your firm. On the other hand the other party may have serious actions which involve compensations, applicable lawful penalties , restrictions of future trades is matter is extremely serious, instructions for stringent audits and evaluation , instruction for necessary organization structure changes when the people involved in the scams and breach are removed, sacked , dismissed . The complete aim of the process is to award the justice and prevent the repetition in future.

- Sometimes when there is gross violation of code of conduct strict disciplinary actions are taken against the parties involved. This is applicable to prohibition on product for public use, necessary testing from authorized technical agencies about the adherence to technical norms, submission of report to review committee and presentation of stand in front of Hon. Court . Due delegation and detailed study happen in such matters and the reputation of the firm is under deep danger. If found guilty, they may need to pay huge penalty and in some case imprisonment.

- It is better to stay in the business with following basic business dealing with trust, clarity and seamless communication. When you report status with sincerity ,it reflect your positive approach , when you complete the product on time , before time , after timeline within acceptable tolerance or even after passing time but with late delivery charges ,it is totally acceptable to customer . But when you supply defective product, the conflicts starts from there. Delay for starting the work for one month to two month which is generally happening delay is quite okay although with little uneasiness but delay after starting the plant because of faulty product is totally not acceptable. Customer insist action on defective part to reduce their production losses which are in lakhs and crores and he has to pay his staff and manage operational overheads from his own earning and profit.

- There is separate way to settle your disputes out of the Hon .court. This stand is taken to ensure protection of goodwill and reputation between the parties. Such compromises happen with wholesome mutually agreeable compensation.

- The time to time amendment of rules, regulations and laws need to be updated in our system with which we can comply the legal aspect of the business. When we are in line with legal requirement we get benefit and information of proposed changes and we can guess the impact of such changes on our business. The tax structure, employee welfare schemes, number of working hours are some point which keep updating and evolving. Now a day, on a click you get all the details on your mobile handset. Compared to earlier days, your major time is saved in documentation and more time is available for actual production. Now you can also carry out tax filing through online mode which again reduced your time in visiting various offices. Because of increased transparency in the system, people are adopting fair business practices with which there should not be any legal concern .

Hope you like this chapter! Let's pause here!

SKILL 194 : CONTROL SKILL

PHOTO CREDIT : CHRIS LEIPELT, UNSPLASH.COM

Dear Friends,

Good Morning & Welcome to yet another skill chapter- Control skill – lets go into the details.

> " Control is allowing right things to happen. Controlis about passing rules . Control is about respecting discipline. "

Friends, control is necessary in fine tuning of our day to day life. Control is necessary to ensure planned work happen without any error and it happen in correct time. Let's see point wise, how control help to accelerate our life and progress!

- What will happen if dimensional tolerances are not adhered in machine parts?
  The parts will not fit with each other and they will not able to perform their design function.
- What will happen if the scale is not mentioned on the drawing and dimensions are mentioned incompletely?
  Every drawing when provided with applicable scale represents unmentioned dimensions which can be calculated or verified with respect to mentioned scale. Suppose a critical recess dimension is missed but if its scale is given we can measure the dimension on drawing can multiply with its scale to get the recess dimension. Hence mentioning of drawing scale is important. Scale act as main control apart from projection method and bill of material.

What will happen if documents are missed and parts are received without its documents? Documents or certificate act as evidence of performing applicable testing. The materials identification and traceability is totally dependent upon its valid documentation. Without document we cannot ascertain the correctness of the material. Here document act as main control of the supplied material.

- What will happen if an alloying element exceeds it value, fail short of its required value or it is added exactly as per the limited value?

  A metallic product consists of alloying of number of elements in a certain range that support the formation of favorable reaction products. When the composition of alloying element is within a tried and tested range, the developed alloy meets its mechanical properties and it is thus the assurance of service performance. When the composition exceeds or lower in the range of composition you may encounter undesired reaction product or higher cost of alloy making. The affinity of every element is balanced by its valency and free energy potential, above or below which its reaction is not effective. Every metallic product is result of balanced chemical reaction with strong bond formation in between molecules of respective elements. Hence any uncontrolled reaction will never form a useful metal.

- What will happen, in a manufacturing shop, there is no quality control and people are working on their own?

  Quality control function for a manufacturing shop not only acts as supporting agency that checks and validates the accuracy of the work but it is open customer representative on which customer trust. Believe, when a good job is delivered, everyone is at forefront of receiving praise and appreciation but when customer complaint arises, it is the quality control function that has to face criticism about the defect or error. The always has to answer – how it is missed from you? Is your checklist correct? Have you checked as per checklist? These are open questions and you can't lie here. Friends, control is not about restricting someone from achieving top speed. Control is not about stopping someone to work fast. Control is not about adding delays and restrictions in the path of fast paced production activities. Control is about respecting the accuracy of sequence. Control is about allowing only right things to happen. Control is about explaining what will be impact on given job is things are not done as per the process. Control is making you aware about the importance of time management. If we carry out things as per process we will go through next phases fast, if we hurry up here, we will be in trouble in next steps which will consume more time.

Friends, control act as checkpoint. It ascertains the tally of whatever we do in speed and in hurry. When we solve question paper and check its accuracy, we get confidence that everything is correct, however when we don't check it we are always in doubt of correct answer.

Friends, hope you like this chapter! Let's pause here!

SKILL 195 : AUTHORITY EXERTION SKILL

PHOTO CREDIT : CALEB WRIGHT, UNSPLASH.COM

Dear Friends,

Good afternoon and welcome to yet another skill chapter – Authority Exertion Skill! Let's go into the details!

> " Authority exertion is about simplifying the roadblocks by applying your knowledge, skill and official grant to make things happen as per righteous way!"

Friends, authority exertion are one of the important business skill which deals with using your power, hold and command for righteous business benefits. Let's see with some practical examples how authorities behave to ascertain major changes that affect business dynamics.

Authority Exertion Skill:

- A batch of product comprising tube length of 3meters is drawn. The actual customer requirement was 2 meter. Because of the unavailability of 2 meter mold, it is agreed to produce tube from 3 meters mold and cut it to required size of 2 meter. Total quantity was 50 No's. Now what is to be done for balance 1 meter cut piece having one meter length and total quantity 50 No's. A new customer is asking for 600 mm 70 quantity, so this set of 50 tubes can be used as 600 mm tube length + 300 mm test piece and balance hundred mm to be recycled as return material. The balance 20 tubes to be drawn separately and provided to customer. Since the composition is same, allocate the heat cast details and offer the same for inspection. In inspection, the material gets cleared on the basis of chemical composition, mechanical test and hence customer accepted it without any concern. The utilization of material within less than fifteen days period was a great example of use of management's authority to meet need of both customers subsequently. Here management discussed this issue with production, planning, quality assurance and after technical compliance and commercial impact they approached customer and third party with available lot of 50 tubes for which customer said he wanted specific grade and size, that's it! Based on this clearance they offered the material to third party, removed test piece in front of them and carried out the testing. The result of testing for earlier 2meter tube and this 1 meter tube came identical as they are removed from same tube.

- In a material purchase from new supplier, material TC was missing result of additional test. Buyer was not sure of procuring this material. The chemical and mechanical properties are available but the result of one critical test requested by customer was not available. What is to be done? Cab we buy this material? Or shall we need to put new order which will take at least 20 days for its fulfillment? The team involving management, production, material and quality function along with design team sit together and they discussed in length about material specification and test scope. The critical test is mandatory as this customer specifically demanded this test to comply statutory conditions of his country. So this is mandatory point. When the matter is discussed with official third party designated for this task, they suggested a via medium. They suggested procuring the part on original Mill test certificate with clear identification and traceability. Then offer the material for practical check testing. Here they will remove test piece as per applicable design specification and standard, they will transfer the stamp and will send material to approved material testing laboratory as per the list of labs given by customer. They will witness the physical test in the approved lab with formal communication from vendor and copy to customer. On customer approval and third party's witness, whatever may be the result of the test; the material will be rejected or accepted. If material meets property, it will be accepted and if it doesn't meet results, same will be rejected. In such a rejection it will be buyers and rather company management's responsibility to return or use the material for other future work where this test is not required. Management seen & calculated the risk in this testing. If material fails, it has to use for other future jobs. But when it will fail this test means there must be some quality concern. So before buying, they contacted a term that if material is failed in test at our end, same will be returned and appropriate charges along with waiting charges will be applied. Two suppliers denied this clause and third one accepted. They checked material in approved lab. Material passed the test and everyone praised supplier's confidence on his material. Friends, authority is all about confidence and honesty.

Hope you like this chapter! Let's pause here!

SKILL 196 : RENOVATION SKILL

PHOTO CREDIT : WILLIAM ZHAO, UNSPLASH.COM

Dear Friends,

Good afternoon and welcome to yet another skill chapter – renovation skill! Let's go into the details!

> *"Renovation is about going with the time , fashion and spirit! When we follow certain trends , we feel to be a part of big team . It gives us joy of symbiosis , joy and togetherness!"*

Friends, how does it look when 93 people out of hundreds are shifted to smart phone and 7 still using the old phones?

How does it look when 900 person out of 1000 buy home and 100 still struggles to find one?

How does it feel when 40 out of 60 student get admission to most lucrative engineering branch and 2- still think about its future scope?

Friends, how it feel when 70 person from a group of 100, achievers their net worth of 1 crore and monthly income of 2 lakhs in less than five years and balance 30 are surprised about this progress?

Friends, renovation are the name of big change. It is not about adding office furniture, glazed glasses and cozy sofas; it is about witnessing a new outlook which goes with latest trend and future friendly decisions. Welcome to this chapter of renovation skills which take into account the effect of new thinking and its implementation in our day to day life!

Renovation Skill:

- When a new office trend comes, everyone grab that change to keep up to date with pace and growth. It is little modification in the way of working to facilitate new way of working to implement desired alterations to have required impact in efficiency and effectiveness.

- When a fashion trend comes, we like to wear new design that matches us and in which we feel most natural and comfortable. The choice of colour, pattern, pairing and contrast everything matters when it comes to following fashion trend. Generally a fashion trend has life of 3-6 months and within one year fashion keep changing and new trend replaces its old counterpart .We have to adopt what is comfortable to us in order to meet going with the trend and also maintaining our own liking and interest.
- Renovation of home is also follows same fashion trend. Every ten to fifteen years, the housing concept changes. Earlier people used to purchase open plot and dreamt of making their own spacious bungalows. As time flee, because of unavailability of land and concept of flats and apartments, people started buying flats. Earlier flats were just meant for normal leaving without much thinking of amenities and community living. Now-a-day concept of township created wonderful outlook of community living in which most of the amenities, daily needs, and important facilities can be availed under one roof. In such a locality, since the everything is available under one roof, you don't have to go here & there and this saves your time in unnecessary transportation and thus saves time. You leave for work and return and you don't have anything to do at home because all facilities are easily accessible in your premises and you can easily go for walk and collect

the things with your preordering through mobile. It is as simple as that. Event though there is any issue with supply, you get home delivery and replacement within one day! What else is required? Townships are planned in such a way that for your every daily need at least two to three options available with you to just go & get the things of same quality , same price and feel relaxed about household responsibilities which is a challenging task for every professional .

- Renovation of vehicle is also important factor. We upgrade ourselves right from starting with normal need fulfilling two wheeler to a descent and dashing sport bike. In four wheeler segment, we first start with simple cars and the move to top model of our choice. Our interest and choice about the internal arrangement of the car keeps changing and we follow latest trend in car designand car decoration.

Friends, we study and then we work. When we work, we get money. With money, we change our quality of life. More money we have more is our purchasing power and more cozy things we purchase to lead lavish lifestyle. But whether other life values which are satisfaction, joy, comfort, sense of belonging and accomplishment are bought by money. The answer is no. We have to work separately on becoming the best version of ourselves!

Friends, hope you like it!

SKILL 197 : ACCOUNT KEEPING SKILL

PHOTO CREDIT : ALEXANDER KOVACS, UNSPLASH.COM

Dear Friends,

Good Evening and welcome to yet another skill chapter- Account keeping skill! Let's go into the details!

> "Account keeping is excellent skill of maintaining track of financial transactions. It helps to increase financial decisions and hence improving our financial stability as well as power to take risky decisions!"

THE SKILL ARCHITECT

When you are an Engineer, you design something useful and create it with using necessary manpower and material. When you are an accountant, you handle the design of your financial system applicable to your work domain. There are thousands of transactions happens in a private or public firm annually. Number of people is engaged in utilizing, diverting, using and adding money into the system and hence a very very clean and keen handling is desirable. Finance being a critical mathematical entity, everything here is measurable and when something cannot be measured in financial terms, it reveals some errors or some financial malpractices. The role of accountant here is to keep track of every financial deal starting from approval of deal by management to auditing of respective deal by both internal & external auditors.

In a digital age, all transactions happen through digital systems and software's. We can raise indents of our requirements, get it approved, float the enquiries and negotiate a purchase order. Receive the material and check its supporting invoice and test certificates. After internal quality approval handover the invoice to material to proceed for financial transaction. Now the finance person as per their area of work, will once again scrutiny the document in the system and will check it in annual monthly purchases. He will check for all commercial details about beneficiary and their tax details. They will sum up the total, check weight, any comment and accordingly sign over the financial statement from organization. Once these things are seen, the financial activity will happen either through ECS, DD, MO, COD or direct payment. All valid modes of payment are interlinked with organizations partner bank or the banks in which organization has savings and current account. Once the financial activity is signed off the same is handed over to customer through materials or respective department to its supplier. The receipt of this cheque or DD is acknowledged and this completes the particular transaction for supplier and purchase end. At accountant end, he has to keep the record of bills received, cheque withdrawn and acknowledgment, same are entered in official purchase ledger book which are mandatory as per financial practices.

Same account is maintained for sales. How many products are sold , number of invoices generated , tax liability and its payment , the payment receipt at sales coordinator and its submission to financial wing taking care of sales credit account . Here accountant has to keep record of every payment made by the customer towards supply of goods and services from your side.

You keep daily track of payments and this activity is mostly done online. Through e-mails you get the details about the payment and even though there are multiple entries, you get enough time to calculate the total at the end of the day and after completion of month, you can sum up the sales figure for that month. When this repeated for quarter and semester you get your financial performance quarterly, semester wise and annual mode.

This business accounting help you keep track of your business status and strategies required to either expand your business or take slow steps about expansion or totally remove new investment from loss making business stream.

Tax liability is major concern when you deal with the business accounting. You can fill advance tax as per your calculations and stay ahead of deadlines. This is applicable of local taxes, income taxes and sales taxes. As an accountant you have to keep close track of tax status and final liability. In the declared deadlines, you have to file tax returns to take care of clean records.

Declaration of profits and dividend to your stakeholder is another important activity. As a finance manager, you take help of your team to fine tune all details and sum up the financial results to management. As a CFO you not only ensure liquidity, business capital and investment priority but also support your CEO is combatting demand-supply variations by making easy money available wherever business need will arise. With applicable formalities you both will take decisions helpful for financial health of the company.

Account keeping skill may be about debit and credit but every penny has value in financial terms. Hence honest, accurate and transparent financial skill is appreciated by everyone right from supplier, purchaser, tax authorities and auditors.

Hope you like this chapter! Let's pause here!

SKILL 198 : BUDGETING SKILL

PHOTO CREDIT : STEVE JOHNSON , UNSPLASH.COM

Dear Friends,

Good Evening and welcome to yet another skill chapter- Budgeting skill ! Let's go into the details!

> " In a restricted financial resources , it your creativity that utilizes the intellectual capability of the people to grow a determined organization! Budgeting skill play an important role in this skillset!"

Friends, whether you are poor or you are rich, you have to follow a budget to decide your expenses according to the life you want to enjoy and the life you can afford. Budgeting skills help to utilize your available resources for fine tuning of tasks in a way to organize your financial decisions, their impact of your current business and future business and need of these capital investments to account for expected returns on the investment made so far.

Let's see point wise how budgeting skill is implemented in different business situations.

Implementation of budgeting skill:

- In a well maintained organization, budget is meant for future development. You have fix order book, you have talented team, you have sound market reach and you have superb business policies. Budgeting in such organizations is all about crafting future business domains and consolidating current business segments . You make amendment for adopting latest technologies, you constantly invest in people training and development , you carry out massive customer outreach drive and always stay connected with your customers , there is system present right from enquiry to post sales service and working with such an organization is almost standard way of dealing with master knowledge of budgeting . Remember there are elite team present to resolve any business issue in least possible time . Its constant source of learning and inspiration. When you spend even two to three years of your career with such organization you will be always sit in frontier row. Because the grasp and scope is huge and great!

- In a growing organization, people strive hard to gain orders. Here you are building your image and hence you have to keep track of purchases and expenses carefully. You have to put caps on various purchases and decide their priorities. The basic priority always lies for purchase of fast moving raw material which is followed by medium flowing job and least priority to slow moving job. A fast moving job will engage your least time in the conversion process and you can expect immediate returns from such orders. A slow moving on other hand has lots of activities and complex operations because of which it takes more time and accordingly same is quoted during ordering process. Here since the process takes time, for same quantity of raw material you invest your money for longer time. Hence in such cases you always insist to receive surplus advances than your regular orders. Customers do agree your demands as they know this is capital purchase and hence we have to support through greater advance which will ultimately reduce of next payment, so it's okay in totality. About salary and service budgeting, you have to rely greatly on your salary time .More is the efficiency of your operations the higher will be output and lower is the cycle time. As soon as you dispatch your jobs in three to four weeks you will receive your payments and once you keep supplying such units the link will follow your progress. In this way a growing organization builds its financial strength through strategic negotiations and speedy operations of fast moving orders.

- In an organization facing financial crisis which may be because of external factors or internal reasons, the complete focus is on urgent & important purchases, quick conversions and constant follow up with customer to reduce credit time. The efforts are made to induce improvement project that will reduce cost , increase saving, reduce waste, will utilize raw material to maximum possible extent , less rework and flexible work environment where everyone can contribute and get appreciated for their support in moving the organization out of crisis. Even small set of items saves lots of amount of money. Big purchases are negotiated for their features and payment cycles, heavy follow up are done for getting material in stock and orders are completed without error. People are aware that if they do not deliver, they have to lose their jobs. And if they succeed it will be feeling of lifetime achievement. This positive work pressure makes them try to their level best!

Hope you liked this chapter! Let's pause!

SKILL 199 : PROVISIONING SKILL

PHOTO CREDIT : SIGMUND, UNSPLASH.COM

Dear Friends,

Good Morning & welcome to yet another skill chapter- provisioning skill! Let's go into the details!

> " *Provisioning is about arranging resources and facilities well in advance anticipating possible outcomes! It is perfect example of skilled planning and assurance of coping with sudden situations!*"

Friends, provisions are made for facilitation. Provisions are perfect example of skilled planning. Provision helps us to deal with sudden situations. Provisions are arrangement of resources done in advance and same is utilized when their turn will come. Let's see point wise how provisions help us to resolve urgent situations.

Situational Provisioning:

- When you visit a site for installation services you always make provision of additional hardware and plug INS. This is because when you are carrying out installation, there are chances that some hardware or some plug ins may get damage and to avoid the delay you carry extra quantity to facilitate quick installation. These parts are very small but if they are not present at the time of installation, our work will be incomplete and hence we always carry extra quantity of these parts.

  When welding is carried out if four welders are working, there is always provision of one or two idle extra machine. In case any breakdown happens with any machine, the machine is sent for repair and immediately the idle machine is used for work. This happens in few minutes and hence the time loss is least. When mainainance engineer check the status of the machine, with his available spare parts and resources, he repair the machine and bring back on the table to ensure availability of two idle machines at any time. This way even though there are repairs, the work will not have any halt and output is achieved in every challenging situation.

- In most of the budgets, extra provision is always done to deal with urgency. This portion of money which may be 10-15% total budget is always kept separate and untouched for sudden urgencies in which regular finance supply is stopped and organization is facing financial crisis. With this fund, major liabilities are fulfilled and by the time issue gets resolved, this fund acts as a medium through which we can sail out ship. Considering the value of this provision being little low, we have to arrange for other strong financial support or we have to sell our business to reduce the liability. But such a kind of provision always helps us to find and buy some time before taking major decision.

- Multiskilling is one way of developing your available manpower for the crisis time. Systematic training programme arranged for your workforce not only adds to knowledge level of individuals but it also impacts your skilled manpower availability in crisis situation. Suppose in urgent production schedule your two people has to go on personal leave and you have to manage the show, then at such times even though you may be a team leader, you have to put your legs in field and direct other talent to take shared responsibility and contribute to performance gap created. You not only provide challenging environment to your staff but you appreciate them when they fulfill the target and meets your expectations. When such situations keep happening regularly, your team is trained to handle such changes and this build important relationship with their responsibilities, additional skills and job urgencies apart from everyone's work-life balance.

- What will happen if provisions are not made? When you have urgency and your regular teammember is not available, who will do the work? You have to plan your resource in advance to have smooth dealings.

If you have not done provision for urgent financial situation, you have to ask other for your help and you have to wait for result. If you get help, then it's fine but if you don't get help, you have to face the problem and you may incur great loss.

If you not done provision for extra machine or extra hardware, you have to stop production when breakdown happens and you will delay installation till you bring new hardware. Carrying extra resources is always a great deal to finish things quickly and accurately.

If you not start provisioning, your planning skills will be in question and whenever failures will happen, you have to think on what could have planned in better way. These lessons are costlier and hence we have to think in totality before planning!

Hope you liked it! Let's pauses! ✍

SKILL 200 : LIASONING SKILL

PHOTO CREDIT : CHRIS MONTGOMERY, UNSPLASH.COM

Dear Friends,

Good Morning and welcome to yet another skill chapter- Liasoning skill! Let's go into the details!

> " *Liasoning is about seeking permissions, approvals and explaining the facts with authorities . It is the best trust building process!"*

Friends, when we are carrying out business, we need various approvals and permissions. There are respected authorities who checks and validates our document and claims, sometime they visit our facility and guide us about the rules and regulations. When our facility found to comply with applicable rules and regulations, we get clearance or approval of work done by that process. If we receive any non-conformance, objection , rejection or dismissal , the impact on business are undesirable and one has to stay away from such consequences to safeguard their business interest. Let's see point wise, as a leader, how the liasoning skill is developed!

Development of Liasoning Skill:

- **Legal Liasoning:** There are laws and we have to obey them. The law details out the ways and options with which the work will be legal. The law also states the unlawful activities and applicable punishments in the form of fine or imprisonment. Law also provides the clauses of bails and how one can achieve justice impartially. Justice is always the matter of proofs, hearings and judgments. When you are true to yourself, it is reflected in your work. If there are errors there is lawful way to attain the error and resolve the matter. In most of the organizations matters related to legal aspect are dealt carefully to protect impact of legal proceeding on business and goodwill. Organization may form a legal department to deal and liaison with judicial matters of the company. Here the appointed business lawyer will always consult you the right path of adhering the law and timely amendments so that you take proactive stand on legal aspects. All your claims and settlement in the court of law is represented by designated law firm and you pay them their honorable service charge as per your terms and contracts. A great law firm always put justice to diseased and ensures you follow rules so that there should not be any legal issues. In different words, they act as your legal advisors to protect your brand image.

- **Financial Liasoning:** In business, as we all know, the need of business capital is met through various sources, It can be IPO's, Capital provided by banks in the form of loans, Your own investments, Your prior assets or foreign direct investment happen in your business. Financial liasoning is about safeguarding the interest of your investors and stakeholders and assuring them best possible practical returns on steady basis for their valuable investments. It is about keeping and growing the trust for prolonged time and in case you sense business slowdown, you must retain their minimum possible investment. The complete fund pull out circumstances should be avoided by maintaining strict watch on business activities. Financial liasoning happens through annual general meetings, financial statements and press notes, networking with financial authorities and their constant support and guidance. Most of the successful business firm takes into account the suggestions given by unique investors to resolve any concern related to dividend and ROI.

- **Technical Liasoning:** Technical liasoning is about adhering to technical codes and specifications. To ensure performance of the product and to assure safety for its users, technical codes, standard and specifications are derived by technical bodies and societies. These codes are approved in assembly house of individual countries after following due process of law and they are harmonized as per international system of acceptance of laws. There are authorized technical officers and specialist who take care of validating the design, construction and assembly of these products. As a business firm, we have to take care of offering them the stages of product construction and adhere to regulations. There are prescribed visit and inspection fees which we have to comply and on successful visit we receive their clearance letter. If there are any objections during visit, we have to clarify the same on the basis of technical clarification and approved procedures. When we get their acceptance, the things move ahead. Building of trust and documentary clarity is critical In dealing with technical experts and authorities.

Friends, hope you like this chapter! Let's pause here!

SKILL 201 : ENVIRONMENT SENSING SKILL

PHOTO CREDIT : IAN BALDWIN, UNSPLASH.COM

Dear Friends,

Good afternoon and welcome to yet another skill chapter – Environment sensing skill ! Let's go into the details!

> " *Response to environment decides our stay in that environment ! To understand the environment , observation, listening and thinking plays vital rolebefore any action!*"

Friends, there are people and there is output. Some environment produce highest output inside the organization or business area while in some environment there are slow track movement and things moves really slowly. There are people in the organization who pull the work milestones and make impossible things possible. There are people in the organization, who stay active and engaged in critical decision making which can last for a month long period. The solutions of our problem depend upon type of the problem and number of people engaged to resolve the same. Let's see how to sense and respond to different environment at job places.

- **_Collaborative Environment:_**
    Here teams are set with mutual interest and everyone like each other way of working . There are differences but there is detailed discussions within the team and they always find resolution for their problems. The active energy of the team is because of the performance they achieve as a team and as an individual . There is independent accounting of everyone's performance based on merit criteria and impact of results. People stay together, work together and party together. When a new member enters in such environment, they make him feel comfortable. They introduce with each team member with their work profile and allow some time to see their work. Here candidate can ask his doubts and with practical approach, their doubts are resolved. This help new candidate

to gel faster and provide quick result. There is equal scope for growth at every level and such organizations are always booming with work orders. Fun at work is important part in such environment and people love having meaningful conversations and chats as they keep working with joy and satisfaction indeed. Just be with the team and your close colleagues, report sincerely and as peryour normal practice and stay happy.

- **_Struggling Environment:_**

    As soon as you enter in such environment, you will see, no one is sitting at their chair and everyone is running behind something. People talk less and they are always seen either typing e-mails or calling their network and customers or working silently on computers. Here no one will talk with each other in office work unless required and the meeting room is also packed with number of issues on board. There are arguments, discussions of errors and losses to business. There is discussion of team's achievements in spite of issues and people stay focused on future needs. When a new team member in such environment he is suddenly given a challenging task. The whole idea is to check his practical knowledge and cultural fit to environment. If he succeeds, he is given more difficult task and this follows till he gets adjusted to function in such environment. This environment always works on new project and innovative ideas and hence there is always rush about work related activities and people are always engaged. The, main advantage of working in such environment is you learn to cope up with work stress and you develop your ability to perform in challenging conditions. You are off course appreciated and honored, but with every appreciation, you are expected to handle bigger responsibility. The comfort zone is less in such environment and hence people has to struggle hard in their life.

- **<u>Non Participative Environment:</u>**

    In non-participative environment, people stay silent and defensive. They co-operate hardly and like to stay preoccupied with old issues and challenges. The decision making is very very slow and there is strict hierarchy through which decision has to pass on. The targets are not achieved and leadership thrives hard to stay in the business. The teams have different opinions and to bring them on common platform, huge efforts are required. The role and responsibility is known to everyone on paper, but in practical life, people wait for their response till they receive formal communication at every instance. Initiative and zeal to work with team is lacking and people prefer to work independently. A new team member always seeks great level of discomfort and he has to ask small small questions since things are not clear there.

Hope you like this chapter! Let's pause here! ✍

SKILL 202 : STRICTNESS SKILL

PHOTO CREDIT : GREYSON JORALEMON, UNSPLASH.COM

Dear Friends,

Good afternoon and welcome to yet another skill chapter – Strictness skill! Let's go into the details!

> " *Strictness plays an important role in adhering to system and general discipline . If you leave things in casual way, they will have deeper impact on well- being of the system and hence they will account major losses!*"

Friends, strictness has its own importance in our day to day life. In our daily life we can remain easy with most of the things that generally happens but for some specific instances we have to remain strict and firm. Let's see point wise few situations in which strictness is important and necessary and what will happen if we denied staying strict.

Important Strict Situations:

- You have availed a personal loan and you have decided to repay it in one year. For one year you have set strict budget and accordingly you plan your expenses. You just keep 20,000/- for urgent expenses, else your EMI amounting to 35000 directly goes to repayment. In such a situation if someone seeks financial support of 10,000, what will you do?

    The answer is, you will promise to pay 8000 in two installments. If the person agrees, it fines, if he doesn't agree, you can say, this month I can give 4000, rest you can manage from other sources. I am sorry. This clarity is required in current days where everyone is preoccupied with major responsibilities and even though they are willing to help, they can help in only a restricted portion.

- You are checking a machined component and its dimensions found to be deviated from given tolerance .The maximum allowed tolerance on part is 0.05 mm and your dimension found to be 0.07! What will you do? Will you reject it or will you pass this to higher authority? The value of part is 5 Lakhs.The question is simple and straight and a strict inspector will reject it and ask for rework When the marketing executive gets the idea about this rejection they may plan to discuss the same with customer. Suppose the actual mating dimension of the part are in possible limit and if some minor rework is possible the part can be utilized with approved deviation and change in part drawing and customer and supplier end and this issue can be resolved. When this enquiry is done, it is found that the mating part is two stages behind and said dimensional adjustment can be done. They have checked the design calculations and there is no considerable change is strength of the part and its stress pattern. Hence this change will not affect any performance and hence same is allowed to pass with approved technical deviation. A preventive action report to be provided with detailed cause of error and same is to be supplemented by root cause plugging at respective suppliers and sub- suppliers to avoid such errors in future. With such a step, the inherent rejection is acceptedwith approved technical deviation.

There is planned customer visit in two days and your documentation is incomplete, at the same time you have to visit a supplier for his approval and you are planning your visit within two days, how will you act in such urgencies?

- At first, you have to be strict and clear about the required communication. Since the two urgencies colliding on same day, if you have to win in both situations you have to ensure clear communication with both team members. Since the customer is our priority, you will check with the marketing coordinator about detailed programme of the customer and the current status of job. You will give fair idea about the job progress and possible roadblocks. You will commit tentative completion time of the job and your bets possible judgment. You will allow some time for response and also communicate regarding supplier visit priority as second urgency next day. After their response you will fix all necessary co-ordination with your team and allocate them individual task. Once the things are set, you will contact your supplier and provide him your standard audit prerequisite to ensure readiness before audit. You will confirm some basic parameter before planning your travel. In case of any shortfall, you will allow agreed time before he confirms the visit. You will give some time to respond and after verification of prerequisite on e-mail, you will plan your visit after customers visit. In this way with the help of clear and strict communication the urgencies are met.

Friends, hope you like this chapter!
Let's pause here!

SKILL 203 : OPENNESS SKILL

PHOTO CREDIT : FRANK MCKENNA, UNSPLASH.COM

Dear Friends,

Good evening and welcome to yet another skill chapter – openness skill! Let's go into the details!

> " *Openness reflects confidence ! Openness resembles transparency ! Its vital skill to understand different cultures and constant zeal to learn new things!*"

Friends, openness is important skill and rather way of life when we think long term prospects of our development. Let's see how openness is experienced in effective business dealings.

Openness at work place:

- Clear and well defined policies are displayed at every central location.
- People call each other mostly by first name.
- There is no mandate to have uniform and you can dress business formals. Occasionally you are allowed to wear casuals suitable to day and events.
- People have informal bonding and they discuss the concerns openly in office premises.
- Confidential things are minimum and system ensures presentation of runtime activities, hence everyone get necessary alert about action required from their side.
- There is regular feedback mechanism and you are aware about current status of your performance.
- People are open to receive feedback also. They listen quietly and work positively on given feedback.
- Customer complaints are minimum and when they occur they are dealt with top to bottom correction and although it takes time, every system step is corrected to avoid repetition.
- Quarterly and annual reviews are well explained and next year's annual plan, order status and expectation from market and team are clearly presented in front of team.

- There is equal opportunity for everyone for growth. Increments, Promotions and Recognitions happen based on current merit and past track record. Waiting for a promotion is just matter of time and challenges are allocated to ensure you are ready for that position in given time. Your high position performance is reviewed by other seniors parallel and informal inputs are given to help you 360 degree all round ratings.
- You are always loved by people for whom you provide extraordinary service. This include surpassing targets, maintain timeline, help each other and appreciate team member, play important role in developing friendly bond with the customers and also cherish the association with old ones. Relationship has major importance and people gel with trust and security.
- When you escalate or highlight a serious concern, authorities listen to your concern and gauge their response based on existing business policies. If they see anything implementable, they promise its execution. If something not as per policy, they convince you in best possible way with which you understand the limitations of given suggestion.
- There are number of informal event with which same work culture is flourished across your organization. In such functions the elegance, style and comfort is represented in open way.
- The general timelines of working are flexible and small delays and stay overs are not accounted. As a

part of meeting deadlines you are authorized to enter and leave the office premises by following normal admission practice in the premises.
- The IT systems are user friendly and for any unauthorized access there is provision of tracing and restricting further access. The zone wise network identification is interlinked and with which all computer system in the premises can be tracked when suspicious activities are detected.
- For official telecommunication, free cards are provided to employees and they are supposed to use the same for official purpose.
- The complete lifecycle is planned in detail to ensure you receive maximum benefits during the service and at the end of the service. It is your duty to adhere to suggested financial schemes which will increase your final corpus.
- The education and cultural facilities are available and with simple registration and approval you can avail these facilities for your personal work.
- Just be there and feel the openness is the normal trend at such places!

Friends, hope you like this chapter!
Let's pause here!

SKILL 204 : COMPASSION SKILL

PHOTO CREDIT : JUDE BECK, UNSPLASH.COM

Dear Friends,

Good afternoon & welcome to yet another skill chapter –compassion skill ! Let's go into the details!

> *" In one of the important human values compassion plays important role . It is the ability to feel the pain realized by others and providing our best possible support to make things comfortable! Its basic spirit of humanity!"*

Friend, we are social animals. We like to talk with each other's, we like to share our happiness and joy and we like to celebrate life events together. The freedom and brotherhood we enjoy when we stay together work together and live together, many beautiful relationships are developed and these relationships act as model of support and strength in challenging situations.

Compassion is the feeling of putting yourself into some ones else's shoes. It is the maximum sensibility and affection one can express towards a genuine person. People encounter problems in their life and with every problem they struggle to get better relief and permanent freedom. The typical phase of facing the problem, working on its solution, bearing the pain and becoming a better person is altogether strenuous exercise. In such scenarios, when people around us watch ourselves and talk with us about the situation and how they can help them, this is the ideal compassion shown by the people.

Every individual can resolve their problem on their own but when there is network of friends, in times of crisis we receive their unconditional support and love which make us feel connected and thus we get additional strength. The group of like-minded individual come together to achieve their dreams and goals of life. In such situations, when one friend experiences some problems in his preparation, the other friend makes things easy for him. The natural feeling of somebody taking efforts to relieve our pain is valuable and such friends always help us to grow along with them . At a particular stage of the life, when all friends meet each other they realize the support they extended for each other and that is why they can achieve current height.

Small things that make big difference with compassions, which are:-

- Talk genuine with people suffering pain. Ask them whether you can support them. If they permit, help with best possible modes and mediums.
- Be present when people approach you for help . General help is sought with regards to time, money or other resource which can fulfill their need and which is available with us or it can be purchased by us.
- Compassion doesn't stand for doing work for others; it stands for being there when they need you most. Generally people who are true to themselves always support each other because they know difficult times are temporary and there is always a way out when we work for eachother.
- A hand of support for a person who just met with accident not only boosts his spirit but it creates hope that my people are with me and I will be free out of this situation soon.
- A hand of support for the person who has failed in his academics gives him confidence to rebound which make him a champion in next exam.
- A hand of support in the form of new orders to a

businessman incurring losses and not getting orders act as emergence of all new entrepreneurs out of him and he delivers with courage and confidence.

- A hand of support to a lady facing criticism abouther working style goes a long way in safeguarding her talent and providing her conducive atmosphere in which she can put her great talent and capability onboard!
- Physically and mentally challenged people are quite easy pick for hardship from society. They have to struggle at every step as they find other people try to fast that they have to remain silent. The provision of reservation is nothing but a genuine way of support to raise them again in same society and prove their mettle. Here every organization has to think carefully and with compassion for every class and breed of a larger society. After all compassion is human value and when we feel what would have been our condition when we would have faced similar trouble make us act with dignity and respect with such individuals and groups.
- Always follow your heart for people in need and your brain will support you in providing alternative solution to resolve these issues.

Friends, hope you like this chapter!
Let's pause here!

SKILL 205: KINDNESS SKILL

PHOTO CREDIT : ROD LONG, UNSPLASH.COM

Dear Friends,

Good afternoon and welcome to yet another skill chapter – kindness skill! Let's go into the details!

> *"Kindness is the value which removes anger, distress and anxiety ! Kindness increases openness and it brings people together! "*

Different cultures has given importance to kindness. Kindness is perfect lighthouse of Nobel value spectrum and one cannot forget its value in current fast paced world. Let's see with point wise details, how kindness act as bridging media in several challenging situations.

Situations and effect of kindness:

It was about 12 PM in night and suddenly four friends started feeling hungry and they were about to search some outlets out there. They were staying in private hostel and a prior permission was required if anyone has to leave the premises for urgencies after 10 PM. The rule was strict and simple. Now since this was sudden situation, they have not informed it earlier. When they spoke to security, they got denial as it is against the rule. Now what to do? One of the friend requested security to please look for one minute discussion with rector in charge and if they deny they will return. After several requests, security guard informed his senior and they discussed the request with rector in charge. Rector in charge suggested that only two people will go and bring the food for themselves along with their other two partners, and the time allowed is 15 minutes. They have to provide contact no and has to fill up out pass with reason mentioned in it. Student followed this advice and they bought some food in late night by nearby hotels which has facility to provide such urgent food. The little act of kindness shown by security and rector in charge made the way for students.

- A team of senior and two juniors was working on project. In the middle of the project, one of the junior faced urgency because of personal work and he has to attend that function for three days. He seeks leave permission and his senior approved it. Now other junior, noting the situation started coming one hour early and staying there for one hour late. This makes him combat the work pressure and this way they managed the show. When the other guy joined the work, they both worked together and in same fashion and they completed the work two days before the committed date. Now theirsenior felt so happy with the situation and they approved leave of other guy to rest and enjoy for one day on account of compensatory extra working in crunch situations. A simple adjustment with element of kindness not only avoided the hurdles of communication and work distribution, but it also enhanced the mutual understanding and respect for each other.

One supplier was so kind that he always used to provide the material worth 1 lakhs rupees to his new customer with 90 days credit. Normal credit period offered to his regular customers was 30 days but for his every new customer he used to give 90 days' credit. This served two purposes. The new customer got confidence to work without pressure and he is sure that the material worth 1 lakh will make him sell product worth 1.5 lakhs with which he can easily repay the amount to supplier within 90 days credit. In suchway, he has supported more than thousand new customers and in which he could retain more than 950 customers on regular basis. For other 50 customers who could not return within 90 days period, he suggested to keep buying lesser quantity of about 10,000 rs and try hard to set your business. Once you set business then you can easily enhance your potential. This joint spirit of courage and kindness acted as big business booster for his customers.

- Kind people have big heart. They always put people and their need at first instance. They solve people's problem by providing them quick solutions and making them easy with their financial aid. Such financial aid act as channel to take quick decisions and by which business momentum is achieved. Kindness is not limited up to certain numbers but which extend beyond continuous support and guidance as and when required. When people support in difficult situation the other person also support in similar situations. Kindness is present in everyone but the response to a particular situation depends upon the individual's affection with other person. If other person is courteous and adorable, people always behave neatly and nicely.

Hope you like this chapter!
Let's pause here!

SKILL 206 : CLEVERNESS SKILL

PHOTO CREDIT : RANDY FATH , UNSPLASH.COM

Dear Friends,

Good afternoon and welcome to yet another skill chapter – Cleverness skill! Let's go into the details!

> " Cleverness help us identify situations and their best possible response. Cleverness help us to talk effectively and take decisions accurately. Cleverness ensures results!"

Friends, knowledge and wisdom are two important aspect of daily professional life. In tricky situations we use our wisdom to apply relevant knowledge or generate our best possible response with the help of in demand knowledge and win that situation. Cleverness can be seen in person's way of dealing with things neatly and cleanly. Clever person offer deal that other can't offer. Clever person interact in descent way that people love to continue the discussions. Clever person in few words convey big message and people trust is as they like it. Let's see with point wise details, how cleverness help people to gel and perform together!

Fundamentals of cleverness:

- Business is done by smart and clever person. Clever people always think ahead of the time and hence they are always ahead of the others. This gives them early bird benefit and new learning's. Even though they struggle in the beginning, they know they are first one who is struggling on the path and hence in the struggle phase also they ensure their preparedness to overcome the struggle.

  The sector in which clever people enter is either highly complex and profitable or it is very hard for normal person to enter and survive because there is high element of uncertainty and still you have to deliver your best by putting best possible effort. The day to day learning of the workplace builds up skill of clever people which they utilize for their business growth.

- Every win is just next step for clever people and they know one basic point that as they worked with process and rules, they got these result. If they have made up some mistakes, they might have stuck in the middle and might need to struggle to come out of that phase again. However this is not happened and they focused on systematic adherence of the system so that they can easily meet the target.
- Every failure follows up to date analysis up to root cause for clever person. Clever person will not feel stable and happy till he overcome his failure. He will never repeat same failure and this mentality keep him record new wins in every sector.
- Clever people always prefer to be comfortable with latest technology and gazettes. They use technical advancement for their growth; in the path they influence their followers to upgrade themselves with new approaches.
- The ability to born every day is the killer instinct of the clever person. They are always hopeful and whatever may have happened in the last night, they collect major points and plan their next morning with bright hopes and free spirit to win in any situation.

When they design a drawing or document, it is reviewed more and more time to account for any errors. When they are through with the concept, then only they release the drawing or document for peoples use. They never release the drawing and document with basic errors as they know it will lose

lots of time and money.
- Changes are easily picked up by the clever people. In fact they always prefer constructive changes. They enjoy progressive stability but new approaches are always on their mind.
- When it is needed, they can easily work with people having huge talent and they share their best possible rapport. Their dealing is easy going and people learn from them many things.
- When people try to fetch them in pool of trouble, they sense the danger by using their network of people they confirm the hidden plan and slowly devise their strategy to counteract with false claims and criticism. This skill is very very vital and it keeps them safe and secure from hidden plans of people.
- The logical approach of resolving problems make them favorite team member. In team when they are with seniors behaves responsibly, when they with juniors they coach and mentor them firmly and friendly, when they are with peers, they share their latest views on matters and find out a descent way out.
- Cleverness is first step towards growth and the growth of clever person always followed with proven authority.

Friends, hope you like this chapter!
Let's pause here!

SKILL 207 : ESCAPE SKILL

PHOTO CREDIT : YUIIZAA SEPTEMBER, UNSPLASH.COM

Dear Friends,

Good evening and welcome to yet another skill chapter- Escape Skill! Let's go into the details!

> " We fall in some uneasy situations. These situations are result of our own inattentiveness and lack of complete preparation. In testing times , we have to face the effect of such situations and devise a properway to resolve and escape!"

Friends, in professional life, we encounter some target and challenges associated with such targets. On one side we run behind the target while at other side we fall straight into some puzzles and trade traps. Making a way out of such trap is not a simple thing and we have to prove our potential at such a highest level where these forces are ineffective. Let's us see, right escape path to emerge as survivor of crisis.

Safe Escape through crisis:

- You have faced a job cut. All of sudden, you have lost your job. What is to be done and how we can escape through this challenging situations? This is the major question for person who believes job is the only way to live their life! Friends, we are blessed with one or two unique skills with which we can live our entire life with passion and comfort. But what happens, in the search of constant salary and better future investment we rarely think toward the self-made path of entrepreneurship. When you lose your job, just sit quietly and think about your acquired skills. Just look around the other business or visit successful stores and get idea about how they manage their regular customer, regular finance and regular product basket. This idea and study will give you confidence that even you can start a small retail outlet with minimum investment and hence you can become owner of your own establishment. You arrange initial money and start the business. It take about six months to realize the optimum level of stock, the month wise turnover and profit coming out of sell of certain items. This analysis also helps you understand the normal business flow and earning expected after putting your best efforts. In this way the retail outlet help you forget job worry and allow you to walk your own designer path of success, comfort and stability!

- In forties, fifty's or sixty's, when you come to know about the critical illness, adjusting to new routine and food habits is always challenging. In childhood we play and study and hence there is no other pressure. As we grow younger we face new responsibilities and hence we give less attention to our health. We change our food habit, we avoid exercise on account of business urgency and slowly we start feeling unhealthy. Only this fact is shown in your medical reports and hence doctors advise you to change your lifestyle. In a new lifestyle you have to cut down your food preferences and adopt new diet plan, you have to focus on regular exercise and make sure you reach weight loss milestones. You start coping with work stress and provide your neat and calm response. After putting hard efforts of six to twelve months, your body responds positively and you find yourself normal range in medical report. This escape path again teaches you lots of old things in new package. You remember your childhood habits and hence love to follow them for your own benefit.

- For a seasoned businessman when one of his business not run well and start generating indications of fallout in near future, he has to think on either stabilization strategies or escape strategies. Stabilization strategy involves funding to business from profits of other business or availing loan for struggling business on the credit of successful business key account. The safety of repayment is owned by successful business and since it group business, everyone has to contribute towards stabilization strategy. People know that in our kind of business such things happen periodically and it is always wise to stay together in crisis. With the received funding, the struggling business and its leadership put great efforts and provide results. In escape strategy, when leadership is certain about closure of business in less than year time, they start accounting the assets and liabilities of the business. Their prime focus is to sell the business to able party if available and minimize their business losses. The settlement of employee and supplier payment is next big thing and they have to take care either employee get transfer in other division or they get good voluntary retirement schemes. The business is closed by paying all debts and managing receivable to best possible extent and legally it is notified as valid closure. This way the escape is planned for struggling business.

Hope you likethis chapter!

Let's pause here!

SKILL 208: INVESTMENT SKILL

PHOTO CREDIT : RUPIXEN, UNSPLASH.COM

Dear Friends,

Good Evening and welcome to yet another skill chapter- investment skill! Let's go into the details!

> *"Traditionally investment is about getting returns in the financial terms but in business investment is dedicated effort input inside human capital, futuristic space and attractive service network!"*

Friends, investment are one of the important concerns when we want to expand our assets. Basically when we think for investment we have some assets in our hand. These assets can be in the form of money or our trusted people who can do business for ourselves and along the way, they also rise. Hence investment always yield some form of good results in the form of either enhanced financial returns or increased service network with which business become simple.

Let's see point wise what role is played by the investment at different times of business:

Investments and Business Dynamics:

When the business is booming, we get lot of financial liquidity and with which we try to create our assets. We buy new land for future expansion, we purchase advanced machines, we try to open new branches, we go on increasing our headcount, we invest in high return options, we tie up with progressive banks and increase our funding, in a booming stage, and we encourage investors to add their investments to get good returns in the form of dividends. Here wherever we go, we see money for business and money from business in pouring inn. We don't have any limitation on selection of talent and we can hire best available talent. All these actions help your business to expand beyond your expectations. This is the best time for your investments and investment done in this time yield descent returns.

- In challenging business scenarios, you try to pick some returns in the form of earlier good investment. Here you have to find balance between net receivables from regular business and capital required for business which is to be drawn from earlier savings. Rather than financial returns, you focus on investment in system improvement which is done with the help of reduction in rework hours, carrying out cost saving project, improving efficiency in the system by adding affordable and indigenously designed software's. To receive orders you negotiate with customers deeply. Internally you try to carry out activities with less profit percentage. With several enquiries, you receive some good orders and this keep you moving ahead. In challenging phase, investments are on lower side compared to booming phase but when you overcome challenging phase of the business, your investment play the role of secure corpus which you can develop in next booming stage.
- Investment in knowledge yields higher returns. Always prefer to study new skills and acquire potential to try them in practical world. Major certifications are valid up to certain number of years but your knowledge remains forever with you and with this you can go on adding future interest and new skill sets.
- Sometimes people also forget investment in time provide us expertise over process. When we practice a task again and again, we get mastery

over it. The time invested by us not only give us the detailed idea about the minute details but this also help us set some fix process checkpoint with which we can increase accuracy of the process and hence we become master of the process.

- Many open spaces become favorable destinations when the development plan of the town is published. It is always advisable to invest in such futuristic spaces. In the initial development phase the prices are also on lower side and this make you purchase more in same money. The return of space investment is thousand fold when a successful eco-system gets developed in ten to fifteen years. The space can be used for either commercial space development or residential space development. Based on the area of location, you have to devise its development strategy.

- There is market up and down and there are big players where investments are safe. We have to study the market trend and accordingly decide our investment preference .Sometime there are major losses on our investments but we have to learn how to respond with minimum damage. The investment skill is basic identity of a successful businessman!

Friends, hope you like this chapter!
Let's pause here!

SKILL 209 : STOCK MARKET SKILL

PHOTO CREDIT : HANS EISKONEN, UNSPLASH.COM

Dear Friends,

Good afternoon and welcome to yet another skill chapter – stock market skill! Let's go into the details!

> *" Stock market skills are important analytical skill need tohave in current business environment. We invest in optimistic companies and ensure healthy returns after duecourse of time!"*

Friends, investment in stocks gives good returns when you invest in right company. Investment in stock is most secure when you invest in star rated company. Investments give confidence to invest to great level when first experience found to be profitable. Let's see point wise details how investment in stocks helps us to create growth opportunities.

Stock Market Skill:

- Under the regulation of SEBI all transactions of share and stock market are reviewed and controlled. BSE & NSE are places where thesetrade transactions happen.
- We have a dedicated bank account from where we can invest our money and accordingly expect return.
- Any company needs money in the form of capital to run its business. When they wish to go public, they announce IPO where they sell some part of shares to public at reasonably low face value. When people invest in such share within 15 days business accumulate the necessary capital with which business activities are started out. These activities involve setting and expansion of business, creating office spaces and hiring staffs, establishing systems and standardization, starting production and designing the details, selling the product and initiating payment cycle. For every quarter end, prepare the balance sheet and tax liability. Declare profit before tax and net profit. At the end of the year, we come to know about the latest share value of the

company based on the current performance and hence the dividend expected on investments. In the annual general meeting of all shareholders the annual performance and order status is shared and dividends are declared. Also investors complaint are recorded and assurance given for its timely resolution. When the matters are related to money, company take due care to distribute it correctly. Any comment on non-receipt of promised money creates legal concerns and hence the care needs to be taken.

- When you monitor the performance of the company for two three years, you decide your future plan to either increase the investment or reduce the investment or keep it at stable size and amount.
- People based on market trend and up-down decide to invest. When market is bullish, share prices goes up and if people have huge stock in such companies, they prefer to consolidate with more shares. When the market is sluggish, the investments depreciate and hence people choose to withdraw the same. Actually if you are new to investment market, when market is sluggish, the share prices are low and hence you can buy more shares, when the market rise up, you can book the profit by selling those shares. This way you achieve handsome returns and your investment proves right.
- The sectors and their performance provide us the direction about investment. Oil and gas sector, construction sector, steel sector, IT sector has good growth opportunities and hence their share prices

are also on higher side. Investment in these shares will give you good returns over long capping period. Pharma sector also recording some exceptionally good performance and hence investment in such shares yield descent returns.

- What to do when losses happen in market? Never worry! As a basic rule of thumb , never invest your all money in few companies instead have wide spectrum of companies from various sectors by which you can get limited but certain returns and even though losses occur they are least . Selective diversification gives best business result in stocks.
- Change in management, natural disasters, political situations, trade amendments and tax structure, people participation in share market influence the normal trading and hence proactive study of trade plot is important before investment. This market study always helps you get good return on your investment.
- When share market is not performing well and constant rise and fall is expected, people divert their investment into MCX –multi commodity exchange market where precious metals aretraded.

Hope you like this chapter!
Let's pause here!

SKILL 210 : ASSURANCE SKILL

PHOTO CREDIT : BERMIX STUDIO , UNSPLASH.COM

Dear Friends,

Good Afternoon and welcome to yet another skill chapter – Assurance Skill! Let's go into the details!

> " *Assurance create confidence about product or service at first instance . When we assure something, it is already seen and checked by us that is the reason why we recommend to others !*"

Friends, when we purchase any new product, we are always in doubt that whether this product work well and whether I will get good value for my money. Assurance is the process with which a product in making is tried and tested before releasing to market.

Assurance starts with product idea itself. An innovative business idea is thoroughly crafted for all its intricate details to check its market suitability. Discussions happen over the creation of branded products out of that idea. People contribute their thought process and further small ideas to make things happen in practical environment. When the idea is approved after due discussion, it is kept on the table for documentation.

This document plans out detailed design and execution process. In design phase the material, construction code and standards are studied while in execution the in built characteristics and their methods of checking are discussed. Check list and measurement systems are suggested to see the status on the go.

Some test and some trials indicate the practical problems during construction. These problems are resolved with required amendments. After final testing the product is packed and released with manufacturers test certificate which give us assurance of method of construction, material used in product realization, workmanship standard and testing scope along with design details. This test certificate act as valid registration document with applicable certifying bodies after which the product can be used for its commercial application. If there are any doubt or errors in certificate, discrepancies are resolved with proper justification and hence certificate found to be correct in all respect. Let's see point wise how the skill of assurance is developed.

Development of Assurance Skill:

- When we take admission to a new study course like a new engineering discipline, we are not sure about its future prospects of job. We want to ensure whether we can get immediate job once we complete our study. The senior student studying in third or fourth year play an important role in assuring their juniors about the branch you selected is fine and the job prospects depend upon your preparation , way of dealing with people and finally waiting for required result when you are facing difficulties and hurdles . These few statements gives us assurance that the invested time and money will be fruitful and it will provide us the way of living.
- When we purchase a new property, the development happening around is not complete and hence we are not sure whether this location will become popular or not. When we invest in commercial property, our focus is tied up with the rush present in locality and the financial status of the masses. Based on these parameters, our future growth is realized. The brokers and the developer

have some key information about future project in that area and possible growth opportunities.

They simply and clearly explain us that how a rupee invested at this moment will give you thousand fold returns in just the matter of five to ten years, and then onwards you have number of future opportunities to invest and grow. This logic is well accepted by our mind and with which we invest in such properties and feel better. The assurance provided by builder proves out to be true and we encourage others to follow their guidance and invest without any doubt.

- Leave professional things, when it comes to have choices in personal life, we take advise of elders and friends who truly know us. These people out of their conscience and our liking suggest us what is truly best for us. It is their assurance for us which make us comfortable in taking important life decisions. When we want to start our family, in an arranged marriage our life partner is mostly recommended by our dear ones because they know that girl or boy since old days and they know this pair will certainly live well and prosper together. When we want to have our own home to realize our dreams, friends and family members assure their financial support and make our home buying decision easy. Friend's assurance act as first step to carry out courageous activities in life.

Hope you like this chapter! Let's pause here! ✍

SKILL 211 : DEFINING SKILL

PHOTO CREDIT : EDHO PRATAMA, UNSPLASH.COM

Dear Friends,

Good Evening and welcome to yet another skill chapter – Defining Skill ! Let's go into the details!

> " The ability to define the status or problem is fundamental ability of a good learner . When you define something, you fix up the scientific relationship which has certain outcome and hencereliability!"

Friends, ability to define the current status or current problem plays vital role if finding out its possible solution. When we see the status, we realize there are number of variables which are free and interdependent. The effect of change in one variable affects another variable in a fixed mathematical way and hence they are relatable. To find out the exact relationship in between variables, what we do, we carry out experiments with finite data and finite area under which the behavior of variables is studied. With noting the trend in data, we ascertain an empirical mathematical and scientifically proven equation which justifies the results for other parameter also. This regularization of relation serves the purpose of problem resolution and hence we can craft out the exact definition of that principle or theorem in best described words.

Friends, let's see point wise, which are the critical points that make defining skill a specialty.

Defining Skill:

- Identify the variables, arrange them in logical sequence, establish their functional relation and present in simple word. For e.g. when we define quality we say, quality is fitness for intended purpose; now the elaborative definition of quality could be adherence to set norms those ensure product performance along with environmental safety. When we define speed, we say it is distance covered per unit time but when we define velocity we say it is distance covered per unit time in given direction as velocity is a vector concept. This way definitions need to be precise and they need to present the mathematical relationship.

- When we define management we say it is an important business approach in which planning, organizing, co-ordination, leading and developing ways to resolve problems is practiced. The aim of management practices is to ensure business profitability and business stability by using relationship between demand and supply in the market. A successful manager has tenacity to run the business in most challenging situations. With increasing pressure of survival , business managers has to take strict call on number of things which include salary cut, layoffs, budget constraint and cost reductions. Here they use the approach of defining the problem statement to find out the possible solutions. The definition of problem statement can be reducing the factory overheads by 20% in next three month with systematic implementation of automated machines. This will save approximately 10% of total expenses done on factory overhead and we can run the shop with descent combination of required maximum manpower and support of automated machines. The investment done in the machine will be retrieved in the three years period and after that the plant will have descent annual saving which will directly add to profit of the company. Here they have calculate the current overhead, the cost of machines, possible headcount in automated machine installation and necessary lay off. Accordingly they reviewed last three years performance record and made a list of poor performers and notified them about required lay off. The bought out new machines and studied their operations. To their satisfaction, they found the required saving and increase in profit as desired. This becomes possible because they defined the problem statement correctly and devised a solution to meet the requirement.

- What will happen if we could not able to define the status or problem in meaningful way? Friends, we will not be able to analyze the things as they look. This will put things in scattered form and this will make our work disorganized and random. If we pick up one issue, other three issues will arise and in the middle of resolution, we will face series of confusions which is difficult to resolve in quick time. To avoid the same, it is required to identify the system variables and note their internal relationship. When they support each other, when they oppose each other, how they work together and how they work independently. This study helps you to set well defined relation which helps you to resolve difficult situation.

Friends, hope you like this chapter!
Let's pause here! ✍

SKILL 212 : STEP CREATION SKILL

PHOTO CREDIT : LINDSAY HENWOOD, UNSPLASH.COM

Dear Friends,

Good Evening and welcome to yet another skill chapter- Step Creation Skill! Let's go into the details!

> " Step creation skill is the backbone of work segregation and its completion . When we divide thework into small steps , we can focus clearly on each step and make things easy to accomplish!"

Friends, a huge problem when divided into small parts, look easy and practical . The ability to divide big problem into small practical step require knowledge about the algorithm with which problem can be solved and which steps are important to make things happen . Let's see with point wise details how step creation skill is practiced in professional life !

Practicing Step Creation Skill:

- When you are developing new product , there is complete uncertainty , but when you brake it in several steps including idea sharing , design , material , manufacture , testing , sales & marketing , you finally come to logical solution.
- When you are carrying out a root cause analysis, the problem which looks difficult at prima facie give you clear solution steps. Here you carry our why why analysis and it end you receive correct and required answer which give us the root cause behind the error noted.
- Carrying out supplier audit located at different regions requires perfect planning and so you schedule your work according to nearest to farthest vendor location. Here in first half, you visit nearby vendor while in second half you keep time for one or two farthest members. In a day you achieve the target of visiting 2 or 3 vendors with proper stage report. For a supply chain manager , managing 30-40 different vendors and getting work done from them at required time is tedious work but because of

stepwise and day wise allocation of work, it become possible.

- You have to carry out survey of 50,000 customers on certain quality parameters across the country and time available is one month. For this task your plan a feedback programmes and prepares necessary survey form. You create a web portal where customer can visit and share their views. You keep survey questions straight and answerable. You along with your sales network distribute personalized e-mails and portal link to submit their responses. You have 100 sales team members across the nation and hence everyone has to send the notification to about 500 customers. So, you plan time of 10 days to send notification with 50 e-mails per day which takes about two hours to finish. Thus systematically you finish sending notification in ten days and allow your customers twenty days' time. In this time, you start receiving their response and hence you receive response of about 49000 customers in less than 15 days, and this way you devise a fast, accurate and timely method to receive response from large number of customer in least possible & practical time by using step creation technique.
- Industrial line production is always follow production in step and series. When a particular job is loaded in the machine, the operator has given the required raw material and they have to produce production jobs in given time. Once set there is no change in the sequence and hence they have to focus

on more numbers and accuracy of their work. There are instances when complete work has to be done by pair of operators in a week period. Here they distribute the wok as per individual availability. For eight hour one team member will provide the output while for other eight hours, the second operator will take charge. This sequence repeats for seven days to produce required output.

- Step creation deals with understanding strength of each member and allocating the potential task to these members. After partial completion of the task, few members are added to group to facilitate next big step. In some situations, two individual groups work on two separate process activities and at the end of the activity come together to join the two separate outputs.
- In personal life also when we have to manage our time and weekly tasks, we tend to allocate special days for special task such as on Monday we will prefer to look for start of weekly requirement, on Tuesday and Wednesday, we will actually carry out planned work after office time, on Thursday and Friday we may visit some friends and family members and on Saturday and Sunday we will have weekend enjoyment and a short tour. Such stepwise plan of week make us happy and energetic without wasting time.

Hope you like this chapter! Let's pause here! ✍

SKILL 213 : PLANNING SKILL

PHOTO CREDIT : ESTEE JANSSENS, UNSPLASH.COM

Dear Friends,

Good Morning and welcome to yet another skill chapter – Planning skill! Let's go into the details!

> *"Planning is first thing before execution. Planning involves thoughtful approach of arranging activities to make them happen in correct way! The result of perfect planning is seam less execution and final success!"*

Friends, planning are very very important skill in our personal and professional life. The necessity of planning can be seen though failed task which takes place haphazard way and ultimately meet with failure. The result of planned work is always certain and it is the consequence of attention to details while doing any task. Let's see with point wise details, the importance of planning through practical situations.

Planning in different situations:

- When we plan for exam preparation, we prepare study schedule as per the priority of paper and allot certain time for preparation. The subjects in which we have quick grasping are finished in less time while some difficult to grasp subject take more time. At the end of the study when we revise the study with practice papers, we come to know the knowledge side and writing skill. We focus on our weakness and prepare more to score good marks. In exam we deliver with same strategy and become successful.

  What will happen if we don't plan for our exam? We will study all subject like the way we want. We will not allot a fixed time and which will create issues in proper time management which is crucial for all sided study of subject. The question –answer practice is vital for writing in exam but as we have not completed study this part may not be completely done and hence we may encounter problem in actual exam . The confidence level will be lower and this may make uneasy situations in exam. Hence your score will be less and if same attitude continues, we will not provide justice to our potential and may struggle for further admission and steps thereafter. To avoid all these happenings, we have to plan our studies in line with requirement of typical exam pattern to remain ahead and become a winner.

In a professional world, when we are playing a typical role, we are aware of the guidelines to follow, results to be achieved, team members with whom we have to co-ordinate on regular basis and the result requirement. When we plan our weekly work, we give priority to urgent task and their deadlines. When we make a schedule in which weekly task are collected along with their action plan , at the planning stage itself we become clear about the result of tasks . This is because planning as a bird's eye view always provides the rough clarity about the tasks. Rest of the things is achieved with the help of step to step approach to handle each task in series or in parallel. When we handle task in series we have to wait for result of first step before moving to next step. When we carry out task in parallel, we are working with team and the final result depends upon team's collective contribution. In the middle of the week when we carry out the review of all task, we come to know about its completion and further time required to complete all tasks. Accordingly we increase our efforts and finally achieve our target with thoughtful action to planned scenario.

When the work is not planned, you are packed with incomplete inputs and all time urgencies. A wide scale organizational mis-planning create material shortages, manufacturing errors, quality issues, payment delay, higher attrition, cultural issues and reduced efficiency as a team . To avoid the same annual business planning play vital role in which team expectations, market response and manufacturing capability is systematically divided into quarterly thresholds of performance which are reviewed at the end of every month. Clear focus is given to clear backlog at the end of the quarter so that there will not be accumulation of pressure at the end of the financial year. The business level planning is followed by department level planning in which important annual task like audits, certifications, calibrations, customer visits, employee appraisals, hiring, relieving and all such activities are planned and executed as time progresses. A successful company always has strong order backlog and in current year they always book the orders of next year. This keeps business cycle moving at stable pace ensuring system, discipline and accuracy. As people are working with stress freeway, there are less errors and more production. Which reduces manufacturing cost and enhances profit?

Friends, hope you like this chapter!

Let's pause here!

SKILL 214 : CORRECTION SKILL

PHOTO CREDIT : ANTOINE DAUTRY, UNSPLASH.COM

Dear Friends,

Good Morning and welcome to yet another skill chapter- Correction skill! Let's go into the details!

> *"Correction are done to rectify errors. When you carry out correction you know two things, what iswrong and how it is required ! When you have this clarity, then only corrections work well!"*

Friends, everyone take care that they should not make error in personal or professional life. The way to correct errors is sometimes easy while sometimes difficult. Correction skill is developed with responding to different types of errors. In fact if you have made errors or have seen how error is happened then only you can correct the same. Because for correction you must have handled the system fairly. If you are novice and trying to correct an error, there are chances that you may create new errors, hence to avoid such complex situation, proper training is given for interested individual to learn details of correction process. Let's see point wise, how correction skill is achieved.

Correction Skill Development:

- Understanding of part drawing is first thing before carrying out correction. When we read drawing we come to know about the part and their function along with their interlinking. When we open the system, we observe an effect is occurring because of a root cause behind it. We slowly go on checking the various input and output and make some combinations in which we come to know the root cause of problem. E.g. when we want to repair a leaked tank, we fill it up with water and apply minor pressure. Because of pressure and existing leak, water comes out from pores and hence we identify location where such leak is present. Once we mark the area, we release water and pressure and with empty tank we carry our gouging of part in which we note some blowholes or some entrapped slag which we remove and then freshly weld it to remove leakage perfectly. We take dye penetrant test and finally again take is hydraulic test. This time there is no leakage and we write and certify a report mentioning the soundness of the tank for further use.

- Sometime correction involves replacement of damaged part. For this, we clear assembly and replace the faulty part with correct one. We check the newly assembled part with applicable testing and clear the work when results found satisfactory.
- Mistakes made by machine are basically resulting because of faulty programme entered in wrong way. When the programmes are corrected, the machines do their allocated task correctly.
- When person make mistakes, the correction happens through systematic training and observation of performance. The review gives idea about the progress achieved and hence further simplification can be done to ensure person has made necessary correction.
- What will happen if corrections are not done at right time? Friends, earlier we correct the things, lesser will be our losses. More time we keep wrong work pending, more losses will be encountered and which will make things messy and difficult to resolve. There is answer to every problem but messy problems takes hell lot of time and make our productive life time

miserable. Hence it is always recommended that we must resolve errors immediately. E.g. if there is error in drawing and if we do not correct before drawing approval, the error will follow through downstream and same will reflect in wrong MOC, wrong manufacturing and wrong assembly which will give us wrong final result. When we find out the root cause, we will come to know that it is error in drawing. Now parts are made with common part drawing, so we have to check for how much similar part the error is repeated and accordingly we have to find out its span. When we trace all parts, we come to total conclusion of the issue and hence then onward make correction in system such as pilot job production, virtual 3D modeling and proto typing to ensure the first part is made correct. If the first part is correct in all respect, naturally the chances of other parts increases to be accurate. This way with right corrective approach we cover the possible risks involved in error in drawings and subsequent implications.

- Friends, our experience make us strong to deal with number of errors and their correction. More is the difficulty level; more is the knowledge grasp we experience while on the path of correction.

Hope you like this chapter!

Correction skill is identity of a seasoned person. Let's pause here!

SKILL 215 : SUGGESTION SKILL

PHOTO CREDIT : CHRISTINA WOCINTECHCHAT , UNSPLASH.COM

Dear Friends,

Good Morning and welcome to yet another skill chapter- suggestion skill! Let's go into the details!

> " *Suggestions play important role in resolving conflicts, difficulties and issues. Suggestions has freedom of usage , if agreed , same can be applied, if not like , suggestions can be returned !*"

THE SKILL ARCHITECT

One of the democratic ways to resolve complex problems in the system is initiative discussions with all stakeholders, put the issues at the center and resolve one by one, step by step by carrying out detailed discussions. Such discussions take enlarged view of the history behind issue, how it is initiated and what was the role of responsibility holders, who mis used their authority and why it is not stopped at that moment. Once this history is clear, the person or group of people responsible has to won the corrective plan. As the part of corrective plan, people put various corrective measures in the form of suggestions. The cross functional interaction always put forward comfort of their own function and responsibilities. People try to pass their responsibilities but in a mature system, people know their own responsibilities and hence they always try to find out what is right for everyone and accordingly they suggest right ways! Let's see point wise how suggestions are given and how they are appreciated and rewarded.

Suggestion Skill:

- We are aware about the decision making process. In certain situations, a fixed action plan is required to come out safely. When the conflicts are going on people argue with each other on their point of view. The opposite party is putting their view which may by correct from their side but as a group it is always challenging to come on same floor. It is the skill of suggestions which brings people on common ground without enforcing mandatory views. When suggestions are put on the discussion table, they come upwith possible solution, clear idea about the required actions and hence more visible to group, some people even show demonstrations with which their point of view is also clarified in details.

- When dealing with financial disputes, people suggest using written record. A written record always notes the transaction amount and the parties involved in it. If you are not keeping written record, there are chances that you may forget the deal after some time and hence there may be issues regarding the completion of activity. This is why bank and other financial institutes keep clear record of every account and every transaction, failing to which financial irregularities will be generated.

- Suggestion of optional material is very very helpful when we are developing a new product. When we have good experience of material ofconstruction, we are aware about it strength and weaknesses. In design appraisal when we observe the suggested material is expensive and a low cost high efficiency material is available, we suggest the material to ensure safety and performance of the product. There may be arguments from design person but as it is just suggestion, they have freedom to check its viability with design calculations and cost effectiveness along with ease of availability and reproducibility. Many times when desired material is not available, designer approach quality person to suggest optional materials. Quality person being well aware about various material codes of construction and latest happening in material world always suggest the right type of material and its extent of testing.

- When a player is not performing well to his proven potential, his coach takes the case in different tone. He spends some quality time with the player and observes his change in behavior and habits because of which he is not performing properly. During such study, some mental barriers and some physical constraints are noted. The coach suggest the development plan which involve reading of useful material , implementing practice drills in which the observed error is corrected , the change in wake up schedule to make the player adjustable with different timings of the game , inducting final match like pressure situations and developing the right response to such situations. This way because of several suggestions, the said player gathers energy and improves in his future performance.
- Friends, suggestions are never mandatory, it's not compulsion, they are always given with clean heart and experienced mind to have better control over situations. Always follow them when you feel they are right.

Hope you like this chapter!
Let's pause here!

SKILL 216 : IMPROVEMENT MAKING SKILL

PHOTO CREDIT : JAVIER TRUEBA, UNSPLASH.COM

Dear Friends,

Good Evening and welcome to yet another skill chapter- improvement making skill! Let's go into the details!

> " Improvements changes the way we do work . Improvement add beauty and creativity to way of working. Improvements increases profit !"

Friends, what is the first thing which is clearly visible when we take charge of an important leadership position? It's nothing but immediate improvement seen in the people's behavior and way of working because of nature of addressing issues and reporting same to our all stakeholders to maintain the continuous progress and ease of working in office. Improvements play the role of lubricant to daily trade mill. They ensure the process and people should not wear and hence they always ensure comfort and profit while doing heavy duty work. Let's see with point wise details, how improvement affect our work.

Improvement Making Skill:

- When we see a process running slowly and creating number of errors on the go, we stop the process for some time, we account the process path, people involved, quality of raw material, machine status and output requirement, accordingly we train our people, carry out machine maintenance, check the raw material before processing and then wait for production trials. The first step output is measured and tested as per the specified procedure. The errors noted during testing are again removed by changing process parameter after noting the root causes. This way in second trial, we observe increase in accuracy and perfection and in third trail we receive increased output and improved product quality. Output, quality and profit follow each other only when process is run as per specified parameters.

If you make process faster, your output will suddenly increase but quality issues may arise. If we make process to slower, quality will surely improve but output will affect. In a practically equilibrium condition, people fine tune parameter in which required output is reached with maintaining quality norms.

- Improvement in design and drawing happens with feedback from customers, end users, internal users and code and standards amendments. Here changes happen with material of construction, strength of material, special feature to existent product, shape and aesthetics changes, color scheme changes, technology integration and latest applications installments. With every change we assure increased level of quality, ease of handling and reduced prices. Many technological inventions are done to improve quality of life by offering range of special products. The transformation of kitchenware from stove, LPG cylinder and stove to microwave oven and sealed gas pipeline is example of continuous improvement.
- Improvement in personality happens with adopting adventures, public speaking and interacting skills. Every public interaction skill increase level of confidence. With practicing public speaking skills and appropriate reading we increase the interacting potential and effectiveness of our talk. When speech is supported by practical data, people believe easily and it increases your credibility as genuine speaker and trustworthy leader.

- When you think to carry out an improvement, you have existing process or existing opinions of doing work. People are used to work with this way and changes are rarely happen. With increasing work pressure, such slower process could not provide result hence there is pressure about some improvement. Such improvement happens with induction of latest technology which is capable of transforming workplace. How many of us know when computer reached bank and other offices , with some dedicated training programmes , people acquired the necessary skill and now they are able to cope with increased customer base and their rising expectations. In coming future, because of huge population, use of technology will widely increase and because of which improving frequently will become norm for a successful person. If you adopt simple living, survival will be difficult until a major social security programme is available. This is because with limited resources and huge population, demand- supply gap will widen and it will make life challenging in terms of required efforts. We have to grasp latest learning skills and adopt communication practices with which we can sell our product and stay in the business.

Friends, hope you like this chapter!
Let's pause here! ✍

SKILL 217 : TRACKING SKILL

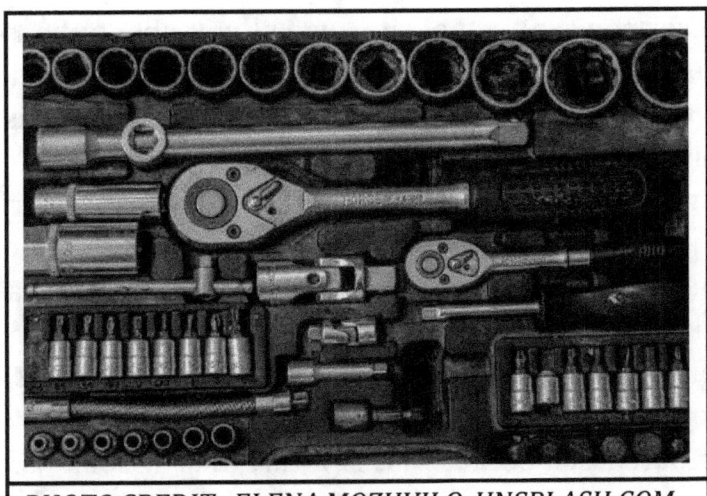

PHOTO CREDIT : ELENA MOZHVILO, UNSPLASH.COM

Dear Friends,

Good Evening and welcome to yet another skill chapter- Tracking Skill! Let's go into the details!

> *"Tracking skill is helpful in noting status of important activities. If tracking is not done properly, there are chances of miss out, error and delays!"*

Friends, quality assurance and control function deals with certification of product. The product and its documentation are equally important. If a product is created and if its production documents are not created along, when issues will arise during product performance at actual site, we will not able to find out the reason of the error and hence the immediate solution to problem. This is why every product has its construction manual plus user instruction manual which help to track the place of manufacture, country of manufacture, the serial and batch number of product and expiry date of product. With this aid, we can easily trace out its in-house testing record in a way to clarify doubts about its performance. Not only this, the use of identification and traceability help to create trust with its purchaser because he is aware that if some issues arises he has some key information on the basis of which he can contact with its supplier . Let's see point wise how the tracking skill is used to ensure status of the job progress.

Tracking Skill Development:

- When we track the material offering and allocation status to a job, we get idea about the material consumption, its range of serialnumber, the unit for which it is allocated and balance scope of material with respect to complete material. When people ask about product delivery date in typical industrial environment, issue of complete material is first step to commit final date of dispatch. This is quite obvious because of material is not available at required time, how can the product complete in time? Hence every attempt is made to arrange the material in time. Once 100% material is available in hand, the rest things are its processing and assembly which is done in comparatively lesser period of time. Once material is available, the commitment of product delivery is certain and if issues related to rework doesn't occur, it can be supplied even before committed date. So a production manager always has to keep close follow up with material planner, purchase manager and apex management related to material availability. If the product is not delivered in time then only production manager cannot be held accountable. For same reason day to day tracking of required material as per production plan and its sharing with concern team member plays significant role. Here tracking skill help to immediately highlight the balance material.

- Payments and receivables are other important factors which need daily tracking. Every business carries out multiple financial transactions in one day. Every finance team member with their available ledger keep the track of amount credit and amount withdrawn under different business heads. This data consist of name of person, his/her department amount credited/ withdrawn, the date and time, signature of issuer and depositor. Keeping the track of these, the typical cash flow in peak business period and normal business period. Also the order receipt status and demand analysis can be done with the help of financial tracker because of which strategic business decisions can be taken.

- When false claim are done because of internal misunderstanding, the data maintained with the help of performance tracker give us a supporting hand to put our side in front of the people. When people could see your explanation with the help of data available, things get clear and you don't have to face further criticism. Even though if sometime the data is against you, you have the clear idea about where to carry out desired improvement. No one can say there is lots of error from your side. People will say these are four or five errors which need to be corrected. So keeping the track of our regular performance not only help us to stay organized and aligned with our duty and performance standard but also help us to defend and protect in times of criticism . Initially it is bit difficult to keep track of every small thing. But as soon as you train your mind and prepare formats of different tracker, then it is only about putting figures as they happen on the go. With tracking you are always in line with physical activities of your work and hence you report status exactly.

Friends, hope you like this chapter!
Let's pause here

SKILL 218 : EMOTIONAL INTELLIGENCE SKILL

PHOTO CREDIT : SAM MOQADAM , UNSPLASH.COM

Dear Friends,

Good Evening and welcome to yet another skill chapter- Emotional Intelligence skill! Let's go into the details!

> " *Modern leadership is about understanding the strength of your team and support , consult and mentor them in times of crisis. The emotional intelligence skill help to know and work with your team thoroughly, happily and regularly!"*

Friend, is it easy to handle team of 20 Engineers, 100 workmen, 7 board member and 200 customers for a single person known as Managing Director or CEO?

How these special profile function so effectively amidst the chaos of competition, political changes, business dynamic and general social changes which keep happening day by day?

What is the special energy that attracts them to work relentlessly and constantly to provide results?

Is handing and working at leadership position is easy?

Friends, answers to these questions have one basic thread –its wonderful ability of Emotional Intelligence. Basically every human being has natural aptitude which makes him expert in handling daily calculation and mathematical applications. Because of aptitude, one can easily think, calculate, decide and arrange things easily. But what about emotional intelligence. It is the intelligence one can show or express in situations which test our emotional maturity, stability and ability. Let's see with point wise details, how emotional intelligence works in different situations.

Emotional Intelligence Skill:

- Suppose you are handling an important assignment and a colleague faces some personal issue because of which he has to leave for four to five days. You don't have any supporting hand and customer is visiting next week. What will you do? As a good person with strong emotional intelligence, you will collect the status about the work done so far and think for necessary planning. You will check in the office if any colleague has low priority work now and can he join him for one day. Even if three people join him for one day, he can stretch for other two days on his own and with this way they can achieve the target in time and also help our colleague to focus on his current priority. Such treatment help to create positive work culture and people realize that working in such environment is fun and even though there are important timelines our personal priorities are given equal importance. Such priorities never club always with urgent situations. These are once in a year kind of thing and hence it's perfectly oaky to adjust such joint urgencies with compassion, care and support. These emotional aspects are very very helpful and this is the identity of a humane leader and mass leader.

As you grow in the organization and as organization grows with market presence, your role gets shifted from a candidate to a mentor. Now you have to do less physical work and more interpersonal association with team working with you. This association requires clear and transparent communication with team to give them fair idea about target. Discussing the in hand issues and helps them to initiate talk with concern team members. Always keep talking casual tings even though you are working in stressed situations. This keep environment warm and happy. Happiness has power to create light moment in which you work without any pressure and also enjoy your work. Creation of informal work environment and giving complete freedom to your team by trusting their abilities and even allowing them openly to make mistakes and learn from these mistakes make them more responsible, reliable and enthusiastic. When your team know, even though we fail, no one is going to scold us provide a feeling of security and openness. Friends, when we hire qualified staff, there are chances that few things will miss in the initial adjustment period. This is the time where we have to do some hand holding, some inspiring talk, and some brotherly advice about how to do things. Once people understand there is so much transparency, trust and support in the system, next time when they are in doubt they always clear their doubt and then approach work. This doubt clearing is also one or two times work. People get aware about performance culture and hence learn through common group sharing which happens over formal meeting or informal chats. This keeps our emotional intelligence skill to highest level desired.

Friends,hope you like the chapter!

Let's pause here!

SKILL 219: STRENGTH BUILDING SKILL

PHOTO CREDIT : SAM MOQADAM, UNSPLASH.COM

Dear Friends,

Good Morning and welcome to yet another skill chapter- Strength Building Skill! Let's go into the details!

> *" Strength building means developing our physical, mental and spiritual capacity while living everyday life and working on it in a systematic manner!"*

Friends, strength are fundamental success factor which help to achieve greater heights in our life! Human being has inherent capacity to express themselves with the help of five sensory organs. The strength of individual is nothing but the consolidated ability of these five sensory organs. Strength has many facets; individual strength is basically classified into physical strength, mental strength and spiritual strength. Let's see point wise how these strength is built.

Strength Building Skills:

- Physical strength is built with regular exercise. Exercise, especially which is done in the early morning period, keep us fresh throughout the day. When we start exercise, we keep building our muscles and bones. Strong bones and strong muscles ensure good weight of our body and hence more power to complete the assigned task without any fatigue or delay. The energy one received from regular exercise is immense and it is the driving force behind every successful step. Another important purpose of exercise is to build up stamina and hence stay focused on putting efforts on constant basic. Running, Jogging, High Jump, Long Jump, Aerobics, and Sports like table tennis, cricket, kabaddi, wrestling and kho-kho increases our capacity to chase and struggle. The feeling of win after such struggle is awesome and keeps us trying even after several failures. The result of physical strength is visible in six month period and then onwards our developed physique gives us inspiration to work further.

- Building of mental strength is result of healthy thoughts and good habits. What will you do if you met with life changing situations? The answer is accepting the situation immediately, analyze it, grasp what you can do to resolve it and put your best efforts into it with which you become winner again. Many times we met with situations in which we enjoy excessive joy. In this state of mind we become overjoyed and this also disturbs our normal behavior. So in both situations we have to keep our emotional balance by accepting some common logical points, which are you are getting what you have worked for, if you worked for Gold, you will receive the Gold only. The only thing is time is not certain, you have to keep trying constantly and one day you will be there where you wish to be. We have to always believe in our inherent potential and we must give justice to our hidden potential. But what does mean by hidden potential? It is the strength inside us which we rarely use because of our own doubts, lack of preparation and inability to express in front of people. Friends, always take a deep breathe, open your heart and do what you like to do. Never bother of creating something funny, new and innovative. Anything that creates happiness is always liked by public. Hence try to focus your efforts on happiness rather than means to achieve it. Train your mind to accept good or bad things with same care, concern and caution. This will keep you perform successfully.

- Building of spiritual strength means understanding of our internal ego system and mechanism of expectations on our performance. Spirituality is bets learnt in the presence of respected mentor and these mentors are highly knowledgeable in the area of various human tendencies and way of achieving control and mastery over our emotions. Meditation is one of the important soul exercises where we forget all our sorrows and make us clam and clear by immersing us in deep water of peaceful mediation. Just close your eyes sit in a peaceful atmosphere and meditate with closed eye for half hour. Keep the virtual image of your mentor in front of your eyes and just keep concentrating, number of thoughts will come to your mind, some may be happy, some may be sad, let these thought pour your mind, the ultimate aim of the meditation is settle down these thoughts to deep down to the sea of meditation and keep yourself afloat with a free soul experiencing ultimate blankness, the state of complete joy, satisfaction and comfort. If physical exercise is food for strong body, good books are food for building mental strength then meditation act as major factor in building our spiritual capacity.

Friends, hope you like this chapter!
Let's pause here!

SKILL 220 : FLEXIBILITY SKILL

PHOTO CREDIT : ALLORA GRIFFITHS, UNSPLASH.COM

Dear Friends,

Good Morning and welcome to yet another skill chapter -Flexibility Skill! Let's go into the details!

> *" Flexibility is the ability of a person to adjust to situation . Its more about accepting harmonious stands and not about losing self-respect !"*

Friends, in life we come across some situations in which we have to take some stands which are exactly opposite to our normal inclinations. Flexibility is one such skill required for every individual by which they can manage some challenging times before regaining their normal environment around them. Let's see with point wise details, how flexibility is practiced in various situations.

Flexibility Building Skill:

- When there is exam time, we wake up early and continue study for long hours. The complete purpose is to have fair practice of all subjects and hence give more time for its preparation. Our normal wake up time can be around 6-7 am in the morning but when there is exam pressure we adjust our schedule accordingly. Our physical and mental capability helps us to study relentlessly in these practice hours and hence become a good learner!
- In a typical march end situation, when there is tremendous work load, we have to make certain changes to completion of our target. We scheduleour activities and break it into weekly milestones. Every day we ensure that days target is met. The thing is simple; we have to work hard till we achieve that target. All team members follow this routing and there is synergy flowing in the shop floor and office space. Because of this flexibility, we work more than our normal hours of working and also get rewarded for our performance at the end of the year. Such stands are most common at the month end situation and we

always wish to start New Year with bang, pouring more orders in our path as we have shown our capability to fulfill the target with clear approach and hard efforts.

- Can you work as quality head in metal industry if you have welding expertise in earlier organizations? Friends, here situation involves great deal of flexibility. You are currently working in welding industry. Which is a process industry? You have received offer for metal industry, which is primary industry. The shift from process industry to primary industry require knowledge acquisition of metal making , list of raw materials , process of metal forming and its quality control test , apart from this technical knowledge, you have to build peoplemanagement skill which involve consultation, guidance, supervision , supporting your team to resolve their problems . Everyone has experience but the challenges which your team faces may need your help and attention. So, you have to use your technical expertise in resolving peoples doubt. When you are in a leadership position, you have to manage other aspect of team, which involves equal opportunity to all members, fair treatment and support in crisis,you have to keep yourself available all the crucial time so decision making will be correct. If earlier you have worked as individual contributor and if you get chance to lead, its big change and you have to open up your personality to think of other along with your own progress. Because your performance is measured with progress done by your team under your leadership. Hence you have to always accept the approach of flexibility. This may involve giving flexible work hours to team, asking more about result and rest things can be left with individual, building a culture of inspiration and self-belief, people should be eager to take responsibilities and hence they need to be appreciated for their contribution. You have to improve yourself from a clever individual to great leader. This transformation is not easy and you have to adopt modern people management skill to work smoothly.

- A person with multiple talents is best example of flexibility. You can be an engineer working in a nine to five job and can sing good song or play violin in the evening. You can be a good cricketer and also take part in quiz competition. There should not be any skill which you don't know! You regularly keep reinventing yourself and always find solace through additional skills. This habit of learning new things requires great amount of flexibility. Once it achieved, you become winner of your life. With increasing level of work expectations, you need to possess this skill at earliest!

Friends, hope you like this chapter.
Let's pause here!

SKILL 221: LARGER THAN LIFE SKILL

PHOTO CREDIT : TREVOR MCGOWAN, UNSPLASH.COM

Dear Friends,

Good Morning and welcome to yet another skill chapter – Larger than life skill! Let's go into the details!

> " Life always give us chance to explore our full potential. The moment we surpass our own limitations and achieves what we have thought for ourselves , we become larger than life for ourselves!"

Human life is full of energy, positivity, curiosity, knowledge and sensitivity. Everyone gets the same environment. One become successful and other becomes more successful. There is no term as failure. Failure is the temporary state of mind demanding more efforts to surpass the barriers of required knowledge, required energy, required enthusiasm and more importantly, required commitment to achieve something great and the best!

Let's see with point wise details, how this beautiful skill is acquired!

- How many of us know about the struggle successful people do in their initial phase? It's one of the toughest moments of their lifetime. They are always occupied with challenges. You solve one problem and other problems await your patience and temperament. Some moments test their ability to believe in themselves while some moments make them feel now we can't move ahead! But when they relax and think for some time, a positive solution emerges as boon and they surpass the hurdle very clearly and effectively. The confidence achieved from such situations is one of the best and this makes them chase the further challenges. With every challenge their internal strength goes on increasing and after attending reasonable good problems they become expert of handling adversities. Now as per the law of nature, greater the risk more will be reward! So, these people always concentrate in high risk area and with their perseverance, they go on devising ways with which these risks become well known and can be dealt easily. Once you become familiar with handling risk, it creates your unique identity and special place in the heart of daredevils! You start receiving challenging opportunities, roles and rewards and as you progress consistently, you achieve what you wish for. Obviously this make you look outstanding and with enhanced confidence you set new goals for your life and become an achiever.

- What if you don't achieve such height in life, this thinking always make them try harder, Because in their mind they have decided to surpass any negativity with positive approach and clear focus on what are the problems, what are possible options, which options will work for me in this particular situation and hence the amount of efforts we need to put in. In fact, a fair understanding of facts which leads to a failure make us aware about the different consequences and it give us mental strength to gather all our courage and stay strong on our beliefs!
- The image of larger than life person majorly has distinct achievement over a wider audience. These achievements are so unique that everyone is thinking to achieve part of it in their own lifetime. These achievements are inspiring and they also set an example about how to reach over there in least possible time.
- Let take few example! The career journey of a sportsman involves important contribution in important games which make their team champion. This is followed with their leadership quality in their field of expertise. After certain time, they achieve skill to lead other and hence they are given opportunity to

represent as leader. Leader has to sense the situation and provide the best possible response to stay ahead. They play at various locations, they have to meet with hardest opponents, they need to play without crowds support, they have to deal with their injuries, there may be few controversies over their opinions or stands, but they have to go through all such instances to prove their mettle. When all test are passed successfully, you become larger than life!

- This identity makes them more attractive to build long lasting relations. They can deal with everyone. This is because they are always open to conversation and they believe in the power of association. A helping hand in crisis provides more help in future and this makes any difficult thing easy. Last but not least the inner confidence of looking at things constructively plays important role in their larger than life achievement!
- The situations in life always test a person's perseverance and determination .It is seen in the life of achievers that they have surpassed the most difficult situations with ease and skill. This is the reason why the life spans they spend on mother earth become a model for everybody which makes their personality truly larger than the life! We have seen many heroes who contributed to society in most meaningful manner and even in today have fast paced life; we cannot forget their contribution to society.

Friends, Hope you like this chapter! Always stay ahead of your life goals; this is the secret which make you larger than your life! Let's pause here!

SKILL 222 : MOVIE & PLAY WATCHING SKILL

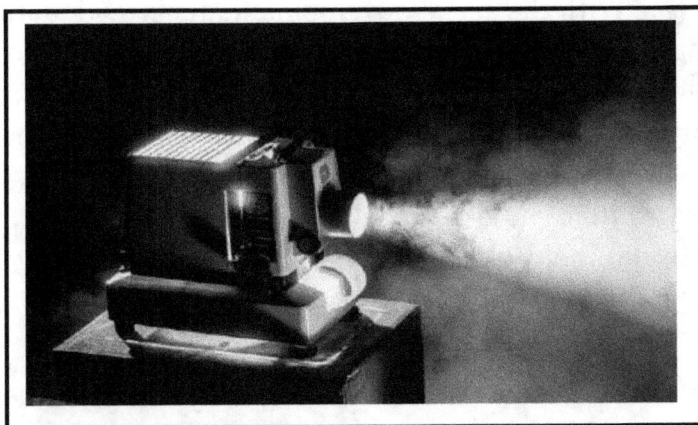

PHOTO CREDIT : JEREMY YAP , UNSPLASH.COM

Dear Friends,

Good afternoon and welcome to yet another skill chapter - Movie & Play viewing skill! Let's go into the details.

> *"Movies are great entertainment activity one enjoy in their free time . Plays are instant & natural performance exhibits which portray different shades of character in a story !"*

Storytelling has its own logic of portraying characters with imaginary sequences of life events. The basic human emotions and their faithful expressions is nicely presented in a movie with mind soothing background score and wonderful pairing of costumes & dialogues to make every scene truly enjoyable.

With the social development and crowd maturity upgrade different adventures themes are tried by filmmakers from time to time. You will think, in this corporate learning book why the subject of movie making is involved? The reason of this question is very very simple. As a best balance between work and life, entertainment plays important role in relaxing our mind, experiencing funny ideas and thinking about possibilities of different imaginations.

Movies has basically four five types, these can be a great love story, a suspense thriller, a historical masterpiece, a classic comedy or a social experimental throwback. The characters of typical period films are presented with enormous human potential. These characters help us to inspire to struggle hard while achieving our goals.

The incidences happen in a movie are fully dramatic. In a specific drama some unexpected things with respect to normal human life will occur in which the lead character will put every possible effort to overcome the challenging situations. This is the punch point where people are thrilled to watch movies.

When a good looking character with his strength surpass a hurdle and when he is equally supported by the rest of the star cast of the movie along with heroine of the movie ,people relate the story to some part of their life. Strikingly this is true because out of 100 scenes shown in the movie at least 20-30 scenes happens in normal human life . This is the reason why movies are known as near equal replica to social happenings!

On the other hand, plays are live display of dramatic expressions revolving around a solid storyline. You have sets, audience and Mike along with flashlights. You have to enter on the dais with your make up and costumes which suits to desired character, you have to start the conversation according to character speaking style and you have to generate modulation of voice in such a way that your audience will remain stunned. The moods of different expression are exact requirement of a descent play. The timing of every act is so important to create the natural feel of the scene .

What will happen if you forget the dialogue or missed that typical expression on your face and attire which is hugely appreciated and liked by audience in last play. This is the crucks of the matter. You have to find out liking of your audience and then you have to improvise that particular scene to make it best selling point of your play or drama.

The plays are spontaneous and there is no retake. Hence level of concentration desired is high. Fumbles may occur in the play but the art of improvisation make the things easy to portray. The commercial success of a movie or play is largely depending on the ultimate chemistry between all characters and off screen support system of able technicians and professional. When the limelight is focusing on lead characters it is very much necessary to check electric supply or make alternate arrangement to run the show without any hurdle. In all way it is the fun of movie scenes which attract the crowd to sit together for three hours with unity and collective affection to enjoy the world of imagination and creativity.

Ultimately as the best actor, best director or best singer is celebrated, the same way the skill of best viewer provide us an insight of creativity and magnified life concepts. When we are watching a movie or play the responses came from our mind are natural and in some way or other it help to keep us active, engaged and lively . When we suppress our major emotions, we shrink our ability to express. When we express ourselves completely, we energies the atmosphere around us. Whatever may be the review given by critics , the one noted by our own heart is very very special and this is why some people like a movie or play very much while few don't like . The factor of subjectivity is neatly learned in creative display of storyline.

Friends, hope you like this chapter. Movie and Play watching skill is a great stress buster and whenever you are feeling low and stressed just enjoy a movie or play. You will surely get new ideas to learn lot of things and magic of life. Many situations in the movie may be shown in exaggerated fashion but the intent of the scene is always providing guidance to deal with situation. We have to keep our conscience alive to pick up only bets part of the story. This is what movie and play watching skill is all about! Let's pause here!

SKILL 223 : FORT AND HISTORY LIKING SKILL

PHOTO CREDIT : PRADHUMEN SINGH, UNSPLASH.COM

Dear Friends,

Good afternoon and welcome to yet another skill chapter – Fort and History Liking Skill! Let's go into the details.

> *"Forts are true indicators of strength of a kingdom in old times . It is exemplary display of courage , valor and pride as far as its relation with history is concerned "*

Friends, history always provide us the understanding of battles fought for our freedom, values and rights. There is always a leader, a patriot, a hero that nation respect, love and follow. The history has songs of victory and defeat as well as it has record of sacrifices done by the great son of nation in prideful service to nation.

In a typical corporate lifestyle when things come to discuss at strategic and thoughtful levels, it is always the various historical evidences that guide us to decide on a particular similar situation. History shows a clear cut record in which if some difficult situations occur on kingdom, how the emperors deal with the situation, what allies are helpful and what stands to be taken to handle the situations skillfully, confidently and with minimum loss to our own property.

As a part of work-life balance, visiting a nearby fort on one of the holiday with your colleagues or friends inspire us to understand the ground level difficulties and hurdles. When we walk across the stiff mountain range in fort area and experience the pleasant breeze the phenomenal atmosphere charge us thoroughly and it make us victorious by shear presence in powerful area.

Let's see point wise how this skill is acquired.

- Choose a spot which can be accessed easily.
- You have to prepare for the best outing and hence take care to pack all necessary material which involve water bottles, sun glasses, tent arrangement (in case you are going to spend some time for relaxation) , food arrangement , caps and loose

clothes , camera , money , a good vehicle , your phone and carry only necessary material which is required for the trip .
- Take account of total distance which is required to be achieved. Break the distance in hour wise target and start walking slowly.
- Always note that it is the stamina that matters a lot in fort climbing and hence always start slowly and confidently.
- It is always advisable to start your trip early in the morning best before sunrise. This help to experience the pleasant atmosphere of dawn and also recharge you with fresh and soothing morning air. By the time sun rises, you have to ensure completion of half of the distance.
- Continue your walk and take pauses in between. This helps you to gather energy after hard work and also provide you time to relook around the beauty of nature.
- Complete the walk in two to four breaks and reach at the top comfortably.
- Visit the energetic and inspiring places and know the importance of every location. When we view fort and nearby area we come to know about its strategic location and the importance of fighting against all odds.
- The compound wall is great way of noting the defense system of that time, which is equipped with artillery, troop and arrangement for war material.
- The palace and museums are great way to learn about tools and tackles, precious jewelries, different

pictures as well as some old time letters written by kind and his associates.

- A fort is not only historical place but it is a geographical marvel which let us know different types of stones and soil present over there. The typical atmosphere on fort is full of oxygen and there is huge silence over the top. If you are visiting the fort in early morning , it is the best place to practice mediation in presence of nature as well as it can be best relaxing site where there will be no chaos , no disturbances and you can easily hear the sound of bird and whistling wind all around . This feeling is one of the best and takes care of recharging our mind, body, soul.

- While returning from fort, ensure you have had good lunch over the top and you have taken your baggage back. The cleanliness is must and we have to respect the serenity of the area. The path of return is always easy but you have taken care of slippery road especially in the times of rain and fog.

- Every fort climbing teach us the importance of ups and downs in the life. When we are climbing upside , we need stamina and energy while when we are coming down after a successful tour , we need control and self-evaluation about the overall experience and need analysis for further improvements.

- Friends, hope you like this chapter. A healthy body and sound mind has the potential to achieve your life goals . Forts climbing gives us the patience needed to deal with most adverse situations of life !

- Let's pause here!

SKILL 224 : GEOGRAPHICAL COMFORT SKILL

PHOTO CREDIT : KYLE GLENN UNSPLASH.COM

Dear Friends,

Good Evening and welcome to yet another skill chapter – Geographical Comfort Skill! Let's go into the details.

> *"Geography always guide us to know about different cultures, directions, natural resources, language and the native people. The networking and connectivity has huge influence of geography!"*

Setting up any business is a special task. When you wish to start your dream business, it is always your natural inclination that attracts the first place in your mind which is followed by the physical place best suitable to business.

Your business card is the identity of your fulfilled aspirations. The centrally located office place always has easy access from any part of the city and hence it draws constant peak of customer form all round of the corner. This help to set your business easily and enjoy good customer base.

The presence of natural resources, the ease of transportation coupled with modes of connectivity fast pace the business activities and hence the geographical location of business place plays a vital role. When you are dealing with international business, the availability of necessary vendor base plays vital role in making sure the availability of site components nearest to place of installation.

What will happen if business place doesn't provide geographical comfort? There are many places in the world which are known for the quality of education available, the industry easily get set up in such places because they get the required talent from that geography. The transfer of material can be achieved with incorporating best transport system but transfer of skill requires availability of huge talent and constant determination. Also when industries are associated with best educational institutes, the quality of research is high and it is in line with current and future requirement. Let's see point to point the important aspect of geographical comfort skill.

- In a typical industry, there is presence of supplementary eco-system which helps to assist big business houses. This means when a big industry comes in a typical geographical location, the supporting vendor network is developed with systematic efforts put up by the big business houses. This development saves time of business dealing, make supplementary material available in time, provide revenue opportunities to vendor to serve and associate with big brand and in turn built their own credibility.
- Any administration provides basic infrastructure facilities necessary for business. This includes good and wide road, 24 Hour water supply and uninterrupted electricity. Apart from this system, the ease with which documentation and formalities are carried out also depends on individual system and the supportive environment for business.
- Certain geography has preference for agri industry while some geography supports software business. When international business houses choose a particular business hotspot, it is the one providing easy access to ports and airports and huge space necessary to start their business with considerably reasonable land price. Here also the inclination of authorities to ease business dealing is important and same is followed in all part of the territory.
- The knowledge of directions plays vital role in business travel. Identification of geographical location with detailed study of direction and shortest path of travel help you to plan your journey

comfortably and ensure hassle free site visit. What will happen if you miss directions? Naturally you will land at unknown place and engage your valuable business hours into searching and relocation. This is why the knowledge about different direction, map and atlas is important in understanding different business places.

- When we settle in new area, the first three month are challenging about adjusting with environment, people and atmosphere. If your body supports to deal with applicable changes, you easily get accustomed with business dealings and this help to settle over there for long time.
- In a typical lifetime of businessman travel plays important role in visiting customers, looking for supplier, developing infrastructure, starting recruitment and hence the correct knowledge of geographical specialties is important to get what you need.
- Geographical comfort is the backbone of successful business network and business relations. Many times it is seen that , people give preference to local people to simplify the business dealings . This is because locals are aware about the culture and trend people follow . There is particular specialty about various regions and buying behavior .

Friends, hope you like this chapter! Here we have tried to cover the importance of business location, local infrastructure & connectivity and the people who make business run with necessary momentum! Let's pause here!

SKILL 225 : FORGETTING SKILL

PHOTO CREDIT : JOSHUA EARLE, UNSPLASH.COM

Dear Friends,

Good Evening and welcome to the last chapter of this skill book – Forgetting skill! Let's go into the details!

> *"Forget the things which are unproductive!*
> *Remember the things which are inspirational!"*

Friends, life are a beautiful journey. We live life on our own terms. Many times in life, we meet with pleasant situations. Such situations give us joy, satisfaction and comfort. When sad things happen with us we feel low, show our discomfort and make things around us bore. The skill of forgetting is useful in letting off things that cause pain and sorrow. When we forget such things , we save important time of our lifetime where we can focus on important task ahead and hence can restructure things which are gone out of our hand . Friends, we can remember things and memories which are associated with inspiration, achievement, celebration and participation. Such things and situations always motivate us. Let's see point wise which are the things which we need to forget.

Forgetting Skill:

- Forget criticism, remember facts, and act on facts!
- Forget mistakes, remember correction done, and always follow right approach at first attempt.
- Forget background, start your relationship with anyone with larger outlook towards life. We meet with some people because of a reason. Always remember why and from where westarted.
- Forget the loss; concentrate on avenue from where profit will come. Plug the holes which are accountable for losses.
- Forget attempts, remember achievements. Every achievement is result of constant struggle to achieve excellence. Hence always feel proud of trying hard

and become successful.
- Forget the past and don't worry about future , just keep focusing on present and what is the best efforts can be done in present to make a path of success and happiness .
- Forget how many time you asked about a particular question, always remember the correct answer which you received after several follow up.
- Forget the initial investment; it is always less that turnover which we achieve after five years. Always focus on five year plan of business. With every passing year, you will grow strong with your courage, sincerity and commitment. Whatever will happen after five year, success or loss, keep putting your best foot forward and always stay positive. Positive approach make you think about possibilities and it removes obstacles of your thinking.
- Forget who misbehaved with you, remember who supported you. Always support last longer than misbehavior. Tolerate misbehavior for some time, when unavoidable, speak gently with person and say with confidence to stop such acts which are not useful to both of us.
- Forget the distance, always remember the journey. Journey gives us experiences of lifetime. We meet with people at various instances and come to know about each other life. In life at one particular point of time, everyone experience similar kind of situations. When people of different ages discuss their lifetime , two things happen, the person who is sharing his feeling feel

relaxed and stress free while the person listeningto it get the insight of life in different context . He also gains life hacks which are useful when he wish to lead the life with mature approach.

- Forget the day and night and just remember moments of association. Association makes us mature in terms of how we love, how we care, how we deal and how we tolerate each other.
- Forget the book and remember the quotes. Quotes come from heart and heart most of the time is true. Always follow your heart when the matters are about people. Follow your brain when the matters are about material things.

Friends,

Herewith I am concluding this skill book.

I hope you must have enjoyed most part of this book. When I was writing , I was feeling excited to share my experience and hence to help lots of aspirant to have feel of life in terms of decisiveness, openness, courtesy .

We have done conscious efforts to keep the tone of the book polite, humble and inspirational. Even if some errors are observed, please share your views and feedbacks at"ppt.inspection3@gmail.com."

Hope you like this chapter.

Let's take a good bye here!

VOLUME CLOSURE

Friends,

Hope you like the skill chapter and overall book structure. We have tried to keep the most informative content interesting and simple yet effective as far as practical skill building is concerned.

As we have committed in preface of the book, we have spread this book into three volumes each comprising 75 skills! The skill wise distribution will be like follow

1) Volume 1 – Skill 1 to 75
2) Volume 2 – Skill 76 to 150
3) Volume 3- Skill 151- 225

Herewith we confirm the completion of third volume.

The chapter numbers of first volume will start from 1 while chapter numbers of volume 2 will follow from skill 76. Kindly take note of same for further reference.

The intent of this break up is portability and ease of reading! Thanks!

REFERENCES

This book is written on the basis of 13 years of professional experience & 37 years of life experience. Which involve experience of study, travel, adventure, profession, competition and leisure activities!

The primary aim of this book is to provide easy access of practical skills and job knowledge to every newcomer, interested individual and general practitioner of Engineering & management domain.

All the efforts are done to present the subject adhering to organizations copyrights and other intellectual concerns.

We herewith express examples given in this book are not to be quoted and they are mentioned for simplification of concept.

For any kind of concern, we are available at

ppt.inspection3@gmail.com

Phone: 91-9970173983.

Thank You!

Have a nice time!

NOTES

NOTES

NOTES

THE END

309 THE SKILL ARCHITECT